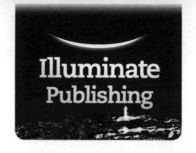
Illuminate
Publishing

WJEC
AS&A2 Biology

A Student Guide to Practical Work

Marianne Izen

Published in 2012 by Illuminate Publishing Ltd, P.O. Box 1160,
Cheltenham, Gloucestershire GL50 9RW

Orders: Please visit www.illuminatepublishing.com
or email sales@illuminatepublishing.com

British Library Cataloguing in Publication Data

A catalogue record for this book is available from the British Library

ISBN 978-1-908682-11-6

Printed by 4edge Ltd., Hockley, Essex.

06.13

The publisher's policy is to use papers that are natural, renewable and recyclable
products made from wood grown in sustainable forests. The logging and manufacturing
processes are expected to conform to the environmental regulations of the country of
origin.

Every effort has been made to contact copyright holders of material reproduced in this
book. If notified, the publishers will be pleased to rectify any errors or omissions at the
earliest opportunity.

This material has been endorsed by WJEC and offers high quality support for the
delivery of WJEC qualifications. While this material has been through a WJEC quality
assurance process, all responsibility for the content remains with the publisher.

Editor: Geoff Tuttle
Design and layout: Nigel Harriss

Acknowledgements

The author and publisher wish to thank Dr Colin Blake and Kevin Davies for their review
of the book and their expert insights and observations.

The author wishes to thank Valerie Burden and Manjiri Joshi for the photography.

Picture cedits; p61: TachePhoto/Shutterstock; p62: Don Fawcett/Science Photo Library.

Contents

Introduction

This book will guide you through the practical tasks specified by WJEC at AS and A2 Biology and will suggest ways in which you can prepare for your practical assessments in BY3 and BY6. Although your main sources of information and help are your teachers, be self-reliant. Know what the specification requires. Use textbooks and study guides. Look at www.wjec.co.uk. This way you can take responsibility for your own learning. Make it a point of principle never to leave a lesson with something that is not properly understood. Many students do not understand that developing the habit of phrasing questions is an important way of learning and testing the limits of their own understanding. So keep on asking.

Why we do practical work

You can read about experiments, watch a video of a dissection or look at photographs taken down a microscope. Doing all that for yourself, however, will teach you more. You will really grasp the importance of bringing solutions to the right temperature for a reaction, you will know the feel of adipose tissue and how it affects organs, and you will appreciate the relationships of tissues within a structure. This is why we do practical work in Biology and why you should take every opportunity presented to you for doing these things.

How this book is organised

This book is organised in sections that address the various types of practical activity that you will do. The requirements are broadly the same in BY3 and BY6 and the slight differences reflect the progression from AS to A2. These will be explained at the relevant place in this book. Each section gives advice about how to undertake the tasks and how to present them when you prepare your work for assessment. Towards the end of this book are sections that describe activities that you are likely to do but are not directly assessed. The table of contents shows what is here. You will find useful pointers in the margins. There are also suggestions of resources to support your practical activities and, because spelling, punctuation and grammar matter, a section about appropriate use of language in describing your work.

Outline of what is assessed

At both AS and A2, you will be assessed on how you design an experiment and how you analyse and evaluate it. This book explains in detail all the areas you have to consider in your experiment and gives advice for each. It then explains clearly how to present all this in a report. As this is part of an examination, it must be all your own work, which means your teacher can give you help and advice beforehand, but for the design, execution and writing up of the experiment, you are on your own.

You will also be assessed on your microscopy skills. This means you must make a well-proportioned drawing of your specimen, label it, and mark measurements for BY3 or calculate an actual length for BY6. If you have read this book, you will know what to do.

Pointer

If you haven't understood something, the chances are that others haven't either so never be afraid or embarrassed to ask. It shows you are thinking and by asking, you are articulating biological concepts. The more practice you have at that, the better.

Pointer

You can learn some things by reading, like how to classify the enchanter's nightshade. You can learn some things by watching, like the courtship behaviour of the great crested grebe. You learn some things by doing them, like culturing bacteria using aseptic technique. Much of Biology is like this.

Pointer

Throughout this book, you will find advice relating to the BY3 and BY6 practical units for AS and A2 Biology respectively. If you follow the advice given here the chances are that you will perform well.

A note on health and safety

The experiments that you do may use corrosive chemicals, such as acids. You are likely to use enzymes, which, being proteins, may elicit a skin reaction. Alkalis and hydrogen peroxide, common reagents, are highly damaging to eyes. Methylene blue will turn you blue, and iodine solution will turn you brown. The list can go on, but it is enough for you to realise that great care must be taken with lab chemicals. Keeping the skin covered is useful but if you do get chemicals on your skin, wash it immediately under running water. Goggles are an essential precaution in some experiments.

You may need to heat a solution in your experiment. If you use a water bath, there is the worrying proximity of water and electricity. If you use a Bunsen burner, there is a flame to worry about and if you are also using ethanol, there is a risk of fire without the usual precautions. Take care at all times and follow standard lab procedure.

When you are given animal material for dissection, it is likely to be a mammalian organ or a whole animal. Some people like to wear disposable gloves, but whether you do or not, wash your hands thoroughly afterwards. While you are dissecting, always point the scalpel blade away from you. Never have your friend hold the material still while you cut. Other people's hands must be well away. If by any chance you do cut yourself, or your friend, hold the skin under running water for five minutes and consult your school nurse.

Always think what you are doing. Follow lab rules and stay alert and aware.

●●Practical tip●●

Even your microscope is fraught with danger. Trailing electrical leads can be dangerous. If you pick up the microscope in the wrong way, such as by the eyepiece tube, you risk dropping it. Remember that school microscopes may well cost several hundred pounds each. Don't break them.

1: Microscopy

When Year 7 pupils use a microscope, they forget to unwind the power cord completely so there is a shadow across the field of view. Then they put the slide on the stage at a strange angle. Then they touch the eyepiece lens and leave their fingerprints behind. Then they say that the microscope doesn't work. It doesn't have to be this way.

Setting up

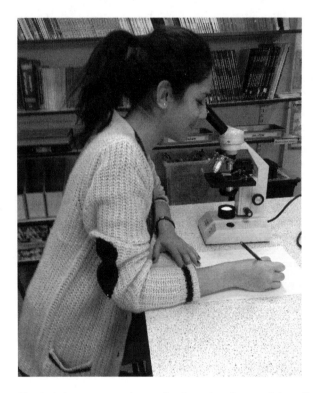

Correct placement of microscope and body. Your chair must be the right height so that you are not stretching or leaning over. If you are right handed, place your page to the right of the microscope and use your left eye. Keep your right eye open so that when you draw, you can superimpose the images and draw around what your left eye is seeing. It takes some practice

Unwind the power cord completely and make sure it is well away from the light source.

On modern microscopes, the tube holding the eyepiece lens is angled. It points towards you when you use the microscope. The power cord comes out at the back so it does not get in your way. Put the microscope a few cm from the edge of the bench, symmetrically, and if you need to, stand up to look down it, rather than grabbing the tube and pulling it towards you.

Use the coarse focus control to move the stage to its lowest position.

Put the slide on a blank piece of paper so that you have an idea of the actual shape and size of the specimen. Then put the slide on the stage with the specimen placed so that you can see the light from the condenser passing through it.

••• **Practical tip** •••

Clean the eyepiece and condenser lenses with lens tissue before you look down your microscope and then make sure you do not touch them.

Objective lens

Start with the ×4 objective lens. Raise the stage gradually until the image comes into focus. Two possible problems:

1. If the specimen has very pale stain, like some preparations of red blood cells, you may pass straight through the plane of focus and miss it. So move the stage slowly and don't blink.

2. If the specimen is hollow, like some plant stems, the solid part of the specimen may be outside the field of view. If this happens, you won't see anything. So move the slide slightly in all directions until you find the specimen.

When you have the specimen in focus on ×4, what you do next depends on the specimen, what you want to look at and the detail you want to see. You can increase the magnification of the image by using a ×10 and then a ×40 objective and, if you have oil-immersion lenses, ×90 or ×100 objectives. Always go up in order. If you cannot focus on an image, go back to the previous objective lens and find it there first. Then rotate the nose-piece which holds the objectives, but without touching the focus control. The image should be almost exactly in focus as you go up through the magnifications.

When you use a ×40 or higher magnification objective, remember to use the fine focus control, not the coarse control. If you use the coarse focus control, the stage will move too far and you are likely to break the slide and scratch the objective lens. Best not to.

••• Practical tip •••

When you have the specimen in focus, look at your microscope from the side and see how far apart the objective lens and the slide are. It will always be this distance for that particular objective lens so remember what it looks like to make it easier to focus the specimen next time you use that objective.

••• Practical tip •••

If you can't focus, go back to the previous objective lens and focus with that first.

Light

Most school microscopes do not allow you to centre the condenser, but when the microscopes are serviced, this should be done. But if you can centre the condenser, do so because it will improve the image.

When you have the object in focus, to improve the image quality, you can adjust the light intensity. Some microscopes have a disc below the stage which has circles of different sizes that let through different amounts of light. You can rotate the disc to select the circle that gives you the best image.

Most microscopes have a sub-stage iris diaphragm. You can adjust this to give the light intensity which produces the image you find most comfortable to look at. Ideally, the diaphragm should be adjusted so that the light just fills the field of view. The higher the magnification of the objective lens, the smaller the field of view, so for the best image, the iris should be adjusted whenever you change the objective.

iris diaphragm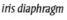

》 Pointer

Objective lenses have a coloured band by which you can quickly identify them.

Objective magnification	Band colour
4	Red
10	Yellow
40	Pale blue
100	White

Magnification

Grade boost

Remember how to define magnification:

$$\text{Magnification} = \frac{\text{image size}}{\text{object size}}$$

Grade boost

Remember how to define resolution:

Resolution = smallest distance between two points that can be separately distinguished.

For a light microscope it is about 2μ and for an electron microscope it is about 2nm, although the microscopes in your school may not resolve quite such small distances.

The purpose of a microscope is to magnify small objects. In everyday speech, the word magnification means how much bigger an image is than the actual object. It's the same in microscopy, except that you can put numbers on it.

The object on the slide is first magnified by the objective lens. If all you had was an objective then the image would be four times, or ten times or forty times the object size, depending on which lens you use. The objective lens also determines the resolution of the image. The higher power the objective, the greater the resolution. This means that you can distinguish two points that are closer together, so a higher power objective allows you to see more detail.

Eyepiece lenses generally have ×10 or ×15 etched on the side so you can see the power of your eyepiece. The image from the objective lens is magnified by the eyepiece, so the total magnification of the image you see is the product of the two separate magnifications. The eyepiece magnification does not affect the resolution of the image. It just makes it bigger. We will consider magnification again when we look at biological drawings.

>> Pointer

Calculation of magnification of image size with a ×40 objective and ×10 eyepiece:

magnification	=	objective × eyepiece
	=	40 × 10
	=	400

Calibrating the microscope

Calibrating a microscope lets you measure the actual size of structures on the slide. You need an eyepiece graticule, which is the ruler you can see. It is inside the eyepiece. It looks like this:

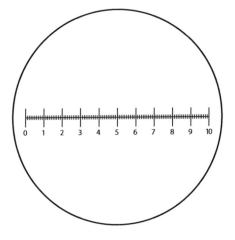

It looks the same through every objective because it is in the eyepiece. So with objectives of different magnifications, the divisions on the graticule represent different lengths. The higher the power of the objective, the smaller length each division of the graticule represents. So calibrating has to be done for each objective.

To know what length each division represents, you need a stage micrometer. This is a microscope slide on which the object is a line 1mm long. It is ruled with markings for tenths and hundredths of a millimetre:

1mm

| 0 | 10 | 20 | 30 | 40 | 50 | 60 | 70 | 80 | 90 | 100 |

•••**Practical tip**•••

Line up the zeros on the stage micrometer and the eyepiece graticule absolutely exactly.

Line up at the zero of the eyepiece graticule and the zero of the stage micrometer, making sure the scales are absolutely parallel. Look along the scales and see where they coincide again.

E.g. on a ×40 objective, 20 stage micrometer divisions may line up exactly with 80 eyepiece divisions:

| 0 | 1 | 2 | 3 | 4 | 5 | 6 | 7 | 8 | 9 | 10 |

0   10   20

×40 objective

Grade boost

Remember to include a key for abbreviations or you will lose a mark:

smu = stage micrometer unit

epu = eyepiece unit

Now three statements for the sums, remembering to say which objective you have used:

At a ×40 objective lens
1.   80 eyepiece units   =   20 stage micrometer units
        $\therefore$ 1epu   =   20/80smu   =   0.25smu
2.   1smu   =   0.01mm
3.   1epu   =   0.25 × 0.01mm
                     =   0.0025mm
Very small numbers of mm are better expressed as microns (μ or μm), so you can complete the calculation like this: =   0.0025 × 1000μ
                     =   2.5μ

•••**Practical tip**•••

Many school microscopes have ×4, ×10 and ×40 objectives. The calibrations generally work out approximately as shown in this table.

Objective magnification	Length of 1 epu /μ
4	25
10	10
40	2.5

You can work out similar calibrations for all the objectives that you use. Microscopes differ slightly in their calibration so you have to do it again for each microscope you use. That is why, in school, it helps if you always select the same microscope. Then you only have to do it once. We will see how to use the calibration in measuring when we discuss biological drawings.

How to make microscope drawings

Making drawings of biological specimens is not art, although there is an art to it. The most important thing to think about is proportions. You are trying to show how structures look in relation to each other. The conventions used mean that when you see a biological drawing you can interpret it in the same way as the person who saw the specimen and made the drawing.

To start you need plain paper and a sharp HB pencil. The lines made by H or 2H are too pale and the lines made by B or 2B become too thick as your drawing progresses. A soft eraser will be useful while you are practising and developing your skill. Rest on several sheets of paper so that the surface pattern of your desk does not show through.

Support your elbow on the table and use it as a fulcrum so that your arm from the elbow down is free to move.

Your drawing must take at least half a page of A4 so practise making your lines long without taking your pencil off the paper. Lines should always look as if they have been drawn in one go.

Like this: **Not like this:**

Boundary lines

In biological drawings, a line represents a boundary. In cells, this boundary is usually a membrane. So when you draw the boundary of a vacuole, for example, the line you draw is the tonoplast membrane, so you draw a single line which must meet. If the line does not meet exactly, it means there is a break, so circles must be completed.

Like this: **Not like this:**   **Nor like this:**

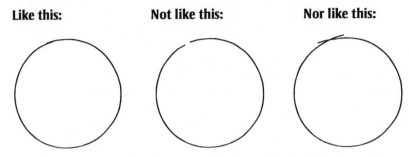

If you draw anything thicker than a membrane it must have two boundary lines. A cell wall is a thick structure so must always be shown with two lines.

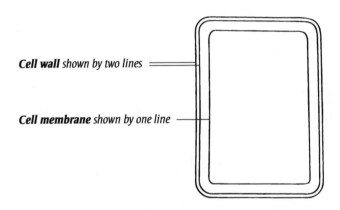

Cell wall shown by two lines

Cell membrane shown by one line

Shading

None. Cross-hatch if you feel you have to, but really it isn't necessary. A line showing a boundary is all you need to indicate the presence of a structure.

●●●Practical tip●●●

Do not do any solid shading in your drawing.

Label lines

To make your label lines absolutely clear there are conventions to follow:

1. Lines parallel, as you can see in the drawing of the plant cell on page 11.
   Although if you have drawn something circular, such as a TS stem, you could use
   radial label lines:

2. No arrow heads or dots at either end of the line
3. Always use a ruler
4. Your label line must end inside the structure you are labelling, not touching the
   outside and not hovering nearby:

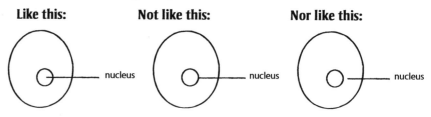

Like this: **Not like this:**   **Nor like this:**

5. Don't let your lines cross:

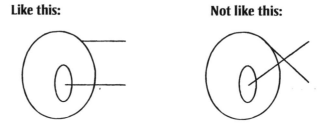

Like this: **Not like this:**

6. Make your label line long enough so that your label is well away from the
   drawing:

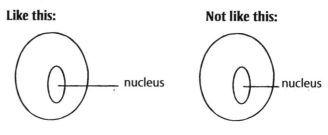

Like this: **Not like this:**

Boundaries

You may draw a sector of a circular structure, such as a TS alimentary canal. It is important to indicate that you have not drawn the whole structure and you can do that by ruled lines that define the edges of the part you have drawn. Sometimes it is described as looking like a pizza slice.

If you draw a leaf section, you should include the midrib in your diagram. If, however, you are only drawing a portion of the lamina, you must include a small diagram to show where the section has been taken from, as shown here. The dotted lines indicate that what you have drawn continues beyond your diagram.

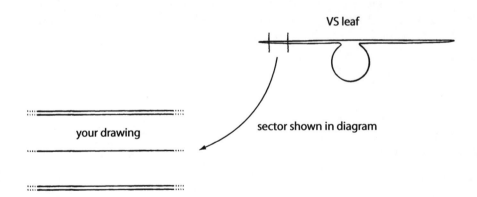

Drawing for AS

You will have to submit one drawing for your AS assessment in BY3. It will be a low power tissue plan of a structure you have learned about in BY1 or BY2. A low power plan means that you are likely to use only the ×4 objective lens. It is a tissue plan, so no individual cells should be shown, just lines showing where the tissues are. Suitable drawings include VS leaf, TS artery or TS root.

If you draw a section through a leaf, most of your drawing will look like several parallel lines at different distances from each other, although, depending on your specimen, you may see some vascular tissue to include. And if you draw a section through an artery, it may just appear to be concentric rings. The important point is that the proportions are correct.

•••**Practical tip**•••

A low power plan shows only the layers of tissues. Do not draw individual cells. A high power drawing shows individual cells.

•••**Practical tip**•••

The epidermis of a leaf and the endodermis of an artery are very thin compared with the mesophyll or muscular layer. They should still be drawn with two lines, as they have a significant thickness (the thickness of one cell, as opposed to the thickness of a membrane) but those lines must be very close together.

Your leaf section will look like this: Not like this:

To show that your proportions are correct, you have to indicate the number of eyepiece units two of the tissue layers take. Rotate the eyepiece so that the graticule is aligned accurately for you to measure. In the leaf, it may be that the palisade layer is 1.2 epu thick and the spongy layer is 2.4 epu thick. Then you must make the spongy layer twice as thick in your drawing. You have to indicate where you have made the measurement and what the measurements are. Your examiner will check that the numbers you have written correspond with the thickness of the layers in the drawing.

Grade boost

There are two choices for writing the actual numbers:

a) Write 1.2 epu on the scale line itself.

b) Put A at one end of the line and B at the other, then in a key somewhere else on the page write A–B = 1.2 epu.

Put the lines to show where you have measured on the drawing itself, not to one side. Draw a little bar at each end, to show the limits of your measurement. Position it exactly.

Grade boost

Somewhere on the page, have a key to say 'epu = eyepiece units'.

Title

Diagrams must have a title. If you have made a slide with fresh material, you should write what the material is and say 'fresh specimen'. If you have used a ready-made slide, read the label and then copy what is relevant, e.g. VS *Ligustrum* leaf. Write 'prepared slide'.

Write down the magnification of the objective you have used, e.g. ×4 objective. This tells the person looking at your drawing how much detail it is reasonable to expect.

Write your name and candidate number.

Drawing for A2

At A2, you may submit either a low power plan, as you did for AS, or a high power drawing showing individual cells. The main difference at A2, though, is in the measurements. At A2, you have to show that you have calibrated the microscope and used the calibration to measure accurately the length of a structure on the diagram.

You must draw a specimen that is related to the A2 specification. Suitable drawings include TS spinal cord, TS ovary, TS testis, TS anther and VS leaf. If you present an AS drawing for A2, you will lose the mark given for the labels.

You must show the calibration for your particular objective lens somewhere on the sheet of paper. The simplest way of calculating it is shown in this book on page 9. Use that formulation to get all three marks available for the calibration.

Having calibrated your microscope, you will know what actual length the eyepiece units represent on the objective lens you have chosen. You can use this to calculate the actual length of what you have measured. For example, you may have a circular structure and have identified its diameter as a suitable measurement. Let us say that the diameter is 38epu on a ×10 objective. Use the following steps to calculate its actual diameter:

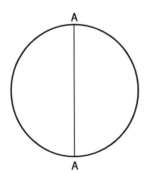

With a ×10 objective

$A - A = 38\,\text{epu}$
$1\,\text{epu} = 10\mu$
$38\,\text{epu} = 38 \times 10\mu$
$= 380\mu$

⏴⏴ Grade boost

As you are writing by hand, remember to underline the genus and species names.

⏴⏴ Grade boost

Go back and check that everything you have written is spelled correctly. If you're not sure, look it up.

●●Practical tip●●

If you have more than a few hundred microns, it is sensible to convert it into mm, e.g.
$380\mu = 380/1000\,\text{mm}$
$= 0.38\,\text{mm}$

⟫ Pointer

Use a sensible number of decimal places. Your calculator may give you nine decimal places, but your drawing is unlikely to be correct to ±0.000000001mm. If you are working in mm, two dp are enough. If you are working in microns, then one is enough.

Grade boost

Your A2 drawing is worth six marks altogether. Correctly marking and labelling five structures is worth one mark. Calibration is worth three marks. There is a mark for the identification and precise indication of a structure and one for calculating its length. See page 18 for more detail.

Units

The standard units are mm but if your structures are small, it may be more suitable to use microns. The way you can decide is if you are working in mm but it starts 0.0..., then change to microns, so 0.034mm is better expressed as 34μ. But if, on the other hand, you have calculated that your structure is hundreds or thousands of microns, you should change to mm, e.g. 809μ is better written as 0.81mm (2dp) and 1257μ is better written as 1.26mm (2dp).

Summary

AS Drawing	A2 Drawing
Specimen related to BY1 or BY2	Specimen related to BY4 or BY5
Low power plan	High power drawing of cells or low power tissue plan
Mark two measurements on diagram, labelled A–A and B–B	Mark one measurement on diagram, A–A
On each line, write the number of epu	Show microscope calibration for the objective lens you are using, including a key for abbreviations
Write epu = eyepiece unit	Calculate the length of A–A, with correct SI units

Labelling microscope drawings

Sometimes, it is not easy to match the structures you see in the microscope with what you have learned from your textbook. The more you look down a microscope, however, the easier it becomes to recognise what you are looking at. There are many useful books which show a photomicrograph and a drawing made from it, with labels on the important structures. Some of these are listed on page 71. If you use a book like this when you are examining specimens, you will learn how to identify structures. The list below tells you important components of biological specimens that you need to be able to recognise when you are doing microscopy, and these are the structures that would be suitable to label on your drawing.

For your BY3 practical you should draw structures or organisms that are relevant to the AS specification and your BY6 drawing should be relevant to the A2 units. Some examples of each are given below. For the BY6 exam, if you submit a drawing of a structure you learned about in AS, you will not be awarded the labelling mark.

Grade boost

Use books like those listed on page 71 when doing microscopy, so you can correctly identify what you are looking at.

●●●Practical tip●●●

In general, you must label a minimum of five structures accurately to get the mark for labelling. The only exception is if you draw a TS artery or a TS vein, where four labels are enough. Make sure your label line is precisely placed, as described on page 12.

Unit	Specimen	Suitable labels
BY3	TS artery	lumen, endothelium, tunica interna/intima, tunica, tunica externa/adventitia, lumen
	TS vein	labels as for artery
	TS small intestine	columnar epithelium, mucosa/lamina propria, muscularis mucosa, submucosa, circular muscle, longitudinal muscle, serosa, villus
	VS leaf, e.g. *Ligustrum*, *Nymphaea*	epidermis, palisade mesophyll, spongy mesophyll, xylem, phloem, vascular tissue (if xylem or phloem not labelled), cuticle, collenchyma
	TS marram grass leaf (*Ammophila*)	cuticle, abaxial/lower epidermis, sclerenchyma fibres, palisade mesophyll/chlorenchyma, xylem, phloem, vascular bundle (if xylem or phloem not labelled), adaxial/upper epidermis
	TS root	epidermis, cortex, endodermis, pericycle, xylem, phloem, vascular tissue (if xylem or phloem not labelled), parenchyma, root hair
	TS stem	epidermis, cortex, medulla/pith, xylem, phloem, cambium, vascular bundle (if xylem or phloem not labelled), sclerenchyma, parenchyma, collenchyma
BY6	TS anther, e.g. *Lilium*	epidermis, tapetum, pollen sac, xylem, phloem, vascular bundle (if xylem or phloem not labelled), area of dehiscence (if drawn), outer wall
	TS mammalian testis, e.g. rat, cat	area of spermatogonia, area of spermatids, area of spermatozoa, seminiferous tubule, area of Leydig cells, Sertoli cell
	LS ovary, e.g. rat	germinal epithelium, primary follicle, primary oocyte, Graafian follicle, secondary oocyte, area of cumulus cells, antrum, blood vessel, stroma, corpus luteum
	TS spinal cord, e.g. rat	dura mater, pia mater, arachnoid, meninges (if individual membranes not labelled), white matter, grey matter, central canal, dorsal root, dorsal root ganglion, ventral root, ventral fissure
	TS kidney, e.g. rat	Bowman's capsule, glomerulus, capillaries, proximal convoluted tubule, distal convoluted tubule, basement membrane

Marking criteria for drawings

The drawing you submit for either BY3 or for BY6 can get you a maximum of six marks. The table below shows you how the examiner will approach your work. If you understand that, you will understand how to get full marks. Remember, it is not your artistic qualities that are being assessed, rather what you do with them.

Only one drawing will be assessed and if you send more than one, the examiner will mark the first one they see, whether or not it is your best. So choose. Don't expect your examiner to.

When you present your drawing for AS, there are two marks available for labelling. At A2, however, there is only one for all five labels, so make sure they are correct. If you submit an AS drawing for A2, you will not be awarded the labelling mark, however perfect the labels are.

Unit	Mark	Requirements	Number of marks	Total marks
BY3	Subject	Low power plan related to BY1 or BY2		6
	Quality	Clean, sharp, single complete lines; no shading; no individual cells	2	
	Proportion	Two measurements marked with value in eyepiece units, with key for epu; correct proportions for all tissues	2	
	Labelling	Correct identification of at least five structures or tissues (four for arteries or veins) with unambiguous labelling	2	
BY6	Subject	Low power plan or high power drawing related to BY4 or BY5 or low power drawing of specimen related to field work		6
	Labelling	Correct identification of at least five structures or tissues with unambiguous labelling	1	
	Calibration	Calibration of the microscope for the appropriate objective lens, in three steps, as described on page 9. Include a key for abbreviations	3	
	Measurement	Identification of a distance measured on the drawing and a calculation of the actual size, using the calibration	2	

Drawings checklist

Level	Item	Details	I have done this
AS and A2	Drawing	The drawing is of a specimen related to BY1 or BY2	
		Sharp HB pencil	
		Paper resting on something while you draw	
		Drawing at least half a page	
		Accurate proportions	
		Lines meet exactly with no space and no visible join	
		Ruled boundary lines if drawing is a sector	
	Labels	At least five structures labelled	
		Label lines in middle of structure labelled or touching line if membrane is labelled	
		Lines parallel or radial	
		Lines don't cross	
		No arrow heads or dots at ends of line	
		Use a ruler	
		Labels away from the drawing	
	Scale lines	Marked on drawing, not to one side	
		Little bars at the ends of line showing precise position of measurement	
		Measurement given	
	Key	epu = eyepiece units	
	Title	Drawing title	
		Preserved or fresh specimen	
		Objective magnification	
		Your name and candidate number	
	Writing	All spellings correct	
		Genus and species names underlined	
A2 only	Specimen	The drawing is of a specimen related to BY4 or BY5	
	Calibration	Three separate statements for your particular objective	
	Key	smu = stage micrometer units	
	Measurement	Calculation of length of one indicated structure	
		Correct units given	

2: Designing experiments

Grade boost

An exam question asking you to design an experiment may be worth up to six marks, so make sure you know this section thoroughly.

» Pointer

The information given here will be useful to you if you study either Biology or Human Biology because the same principles apply.

How to design a lab experiment

When you study A Level Biology, you often think about how to plan and carry out experiments. Just as at GCSE, there is likely to be an exam question that asks you to do that and for BY3 and BY6 you will write up your own experiment. So it is important to know how to apply the basic principles.

General point about units

In Biology, the convention is to follow the criteria laid down by the Institute of Biology, so SI (Système Internationale) units are used. Here are the units that are used most:

	Length	Volume	Time
SI units	1m = 1000mm 1mm = 1000μ or μm 1000μ = 1000nm Notice how easy it is to convert – just $\times$ 1000 each time.	1dm^3 = 1000cm^3 1cm^3 = 1000mm^3	Seconds, abbreviated to s (note to Welsh speakers writing in English: that's 's' not 'e')
Note of caution	cm are not SI units so we rarely use them	l (litres) and ml (millilitres) are not SI units so we do not use them	Use minutes if the numbers of seconds are so large that the human brain cannot grasp them. Make sure you do not use a combination of units and seconds. Use only one unit at a time.

Experimental design

The descriptions below apply to both AS and A2 experiments. Once you have done it for BY3, it will seem much easier when you do BY6. There are five major areas to consider: variables, control experiment, accuracy, repeatability and the numerical analysis. Of course, these sections all have sub-sections. Here they are:

1. Variables

A variable is something that can change. It may be you, the experimenter, who changes it, it may be the different readings you take and it may be something in the surroundings which has no bearing on your experiment, but may change anyway and then make a difference. We will look at three types of variable.

a) **Independent variable** – this is the factor you choose to change. You decide its values so they are fixed and do not depend on anything else that is going on. That is why they are 'independent'.

> **Example:** In an experiment to test the effect of pH on the reaction rate of the hydrolysis of hydrogen peroxide by catalase, you would measure the rate of reaction at several different pH values that you have chosen.
>
> So pH is the independent variable.

At A Level, when designing an experiment, use a minimum of five values for the independent variable. One of the values could be zero. In that case, you would add water instead of your test solution, to keep the total volume, and therefore the concentration of everything else, the same.

b) **Dependent variable** – this is what you plot on your graph. It is what you count or measure or what you calculate from your counts or measurements. The dependent variable depends on the independent variable, hence the name.

> **Example:** In an experiment to test the effect of carbon dioxide concentration on the rate of photosynthesis of pond weed, you would measure the rate of photosynthesis for several different concentrations of carbon dioxide.
>
> So rate of photosynthesis is the dependent variable.

c) **Controlled variables** – in an experiment, the only thing you want to change to get your readings is the independent variable. Everything else about your experiment stays the same so you have to control them.

> **Examples:** If the temperature kept changing in an enzyme experiment, or the light intensity kept changing in a photosynthesis experiment, your results would not be valid. Such factors must be kept constant so they do not affect your results. They are therefore controlled.

 Pointer

Make sure you distinguish between volume and concentration. If you have $2cm^3$ of 1% enzyme, it is twice the volume of $1cm^3$ of 1% enzyme. Its concentration is the same.

If you have $2cm^3$ of 2% enzyme, it is twice the concentration of $2cm^3$ 1% enzyme, but its volume is the same.

Students sometimes think that $2cm^3$ is twice the concentration of $1cm^3$ enzyme but you will not make that mistake.

SAFETY NOTE

Avoid skin contact with hot water. If you are using an electrically heated water bath, take care not to splash around the electric socket. If you are heating your water over a Bunsen burner, be careful around the flame.

» Pointer

Notice the spelling – you chose some variables and keep them the same. You control them and keep them constant so they are 'controlled variables'. The 'control experiment' is something else entirely.

When you do enzyme experiments, there are several factors that can easily be changed. They are:

- enzyme concentration
- enzyme volume
- substrate concentration
- substrate volume
- temperature
- pH.

In any enzyme experiment, one of these will be the independent variable. All the others must stay constant, so if you can remember this list, it will always be easy to think about controlled variables.

2. Control experiment

When you do an experiment and get your results, your meanest critic might say 'but that's going to happen anyway. It's nothing to do with your independent variable.' To prove them wrong, you set up a 'control'. This means you take away the most significant element in the experiment. Then, when you run the experiment, you get no change in the results. In this way, you can see that the change in the results (dependent variable) is directly because of the change in the independent variable.

» Pointer

The control experiment removes a vital agent of your experiment, proving that it is the independent variable that is responsible for the difference in your results.

> **Example:** In an experiment to test the effect of substrate concentration on the rate of hydrolysis of starch by amylase, denature the amylase by boiling for ten minutes then cooling it before use. It is denatured and cannot catalyse a reaction so there is no digestion.
>
> This shows that when you had different results before boiling, it was because of the enzyme, so your results showed the true effects of starch concentration.

» Pointer

Do not use a zero value of your independent variable for the control experiment. Zero is just another value for the independent variable.

If your independent variable is a concentration, don't use zero concentration as a control, because zero is just another value for the independent variable. Denaturing the enzyme is generally the most suitable control.

If you are investigating photosynthesis or transpiration, it is tempting to think about zero light intensity as a control but then you could not see to do your experiment. Also, if the independent variable is light intensity, zero is just another value. So for these types of experiments, it makes sense, when you have collected all your results, to do it one more time with all the leaves removed as the control.

3. Accuracy

At A Level, you know how to use the apparatus properly so we have to assume there is no human error. Only you know if that is justified. This means that the accuracy of your readings depends on the accuracy of your equipment. We can think about this is two ways:

» Pointer

'Accuracy' refers to how true your readings are.

- **Objective readings** are made when you read off a scale and anyone making the reading will get the same answer, e.g. volume in a measuring cylinder, time on a stop-clock. You are limited by how far apart the graduations are.

> **Examples:** If you measure volume in a 10cm³ syringe graduated in mm, you can, in theory, estimate to the nearest 0.1cm³, but you are only accurate to the nearest cm³, i.e. you have an accuracy of ± 1cm³.
>
> If you measure length with a 15cm ruler graduated in mm, you can, in theory, estimate to the nearest 0.1mm, but you are only accurate to the nearest mm, i.e. you have an accuracy of ± 1mm.

- **Subjective results** have an element of your personal judgement, such as when you match a colour to an indicator paper, or decide when a solution has changed colour and what colour it has changed from and to. Everyone's eyes are different and people judge in different ways, so it may be that no two people would agree. So here, the subjective judgement is a limitation on the accuracy of the experiment.

Grade boost

Make sure you know which of your readings are subjective and which are objective.

4. Repeatability

This is sometimes called reliability or consistency and it describes how likely you are to get the same results more than once. If you do an experiment once, you may get an accurate result or it may be a bit off or it may be completely wrong. You have no way of knowing which. If you use your apparatus properly and take readings with great care then every time you do the experiment you ought to get the same result. But it doesn't happen like that in real life, because very small differences in the set-up or timing make a difference to the result, as does innate biological variation. In fact, if you get exactly the same results when you do your repeats, it looks rather suspicious.

So to get around this problem, it is normal to take readings several times. Three times is suitable in an A Level experiment. Then you can calculate a mean result. The mean is more reliable than any individual result because it takes into account all the slight variations that have happened and all the individual readings are scattered around it. The more repeats you use to calculate the mean, the more reliable the mean is. Every time you take a reading, it is as accurate as every other time, but the mean is more reliable than an individual reading because it takes all them into account.

Another advantage of using many results to calculate a mean is that if you get a fluke result that is clearly very different from all the others, you are entitled to discard it in your calculation. That isn't cheating. It is a way of acknowledging that in Biology systems are very difficult to replicate exactly.

What's the difference between accuracy and reliability?

Think of it this way: every morning you get on your bathroom scales and you weigh 50 kg. You eat healthily and exercise the same amount each day so you don't expect your weight to change. And you weigh 50 kg every morning. Your scales are very reliable because you always get the same result. But little known to you, your evil twin has adjusted the scales so that every time, they weigh 5 kg too little. So although they are highly reliable, they are not accurate.

Reliability is about getting the same answer each time. Accuracy is about getting the true answer.

These are not the same thing.

Pointer

Repeatability, reliability and consistency refer to how close your repeat readings are to each other. You might even hear the word replicability, but probably not from an A Level student.

Grade boost

The mean is no more accurate than an individual reading but it is more reliable.

Pointer

What's the difference between reliability and reproducibility?

Reliability refers to the consistency of the results.

Reproducibility refers to doing an experiment another way and getting the same results.

Reproducibility can give you confidence in the reliability of your results but they are not the same thing.

Grade boost

Always use the same number of dp for your results and indicate how many in the column heading.

5. Numerical analysis

A. Decimal places (dp)

The number of decimal places you use depends on how the apparatus is graduated. If you are using a data logger, then you can choose how many dp you read to, but choose sensibly. One may well be enough. If you are using a scale graduated in mm then you can read to the nearest mm and record in whole numbers of mm.

If you are timing in seconds, only read to the nearest second. Your response time and the limitations of your equipment mean that this is the most accurate you can be. So no dp in this case.

If you are calculating a mean from repeat readings, it is acceptable to quote one dp more than you have given in your results table. But don't forget to always give the same number of dp, even if you calculate to a whole number, you must still quote the same number, e.g. 3.0, not just 3 if all the other means are given to one dp.

B. Rate of enzyme-controlled reaction

There are a lot of experiments, especially at AS Level, which demonstrate the properties of enzymes. It is useful to make calculations from your data that show the rate of reaction. The way you do this will depend on the particular experiment.

> **Example 1**
> **Investigating the rate of hydrolysis of hydrogen peroxide by catalase**
>
> You collect oxygen by displacement of water and read its volume in either an inverted measuring cylinder or a gas syringe. The more gas you collect in a given time, the faster the reaction is happening, so the volume of oxygen represents the rate of reaction and no further calculations are needed.

> **Example 2**
> **Investigating the rate of digestion of casein in milk by trypsin**
>
> You time how long it takes for milk to clear. This may be done subjectively, by eye, or by having the reaction take place in a test tube in a colorimeter. Then you can time how long it takes for the milk to reach a pre-decided absorbance. Either way you will measure a time. To convert that to a rate, you find the reciprocal because rate = 1/time.

When you analyse your experiment, remember to discuss either time or rate, depending on what your aim is, but don't get the two confused.

Pointer

Calculating rate of reaction depends on the experiment:

Examples 1 and 4:
rate of reaction = volume

Examples 2 and 3:
rate of reaction = 1/time

> **Example 3**
> **Measuring the rate of respiration in yeast**
>
> Your experiment may be to measure the rate of respiration in yeast, in which case you may be measuring the time an indicator takes to decolorise. Respiration is a sequence of enzyme-controlled reactions and so this experiment can be thought of in the same way as the enzyme experiments. In this case, the rate is given by rate = 1/time. But remember to use either minutes or seconds and not a combination of the two.

When you measure the rate of photosynthesis, you are also measuring the rate of a sequence of enzyme-controlled reactions.

Example 4
Measuring the rate of photosynthesis of *Elodea*, Canadian pond weed

In this experiment you may measure the volume of oxygen produced by a given mass of *Elodea* in a given time. The volume collected is a measure of the rate of photosynthesis but you would quote it as a volume (cm^3) and explain in your analysis why this is equivalent to the rate of photosynthesis.

C. Standard notation

If you are calculating a rate of reaction using a reciprocal you may have zeros after the decimal point. It is perfectly acceptable then to multiply all your results, e.g. by 100 to remove the zeros and have one number before the decimal point and $\times 10^2$. This is called standard notation. It's much easier to plot. Don't forget to indicate that you have done this in the column headings.

Example
An experiment testing the effect of pH on the rate of production of a colour change

pH	time for indicator to change colour /s	reaction rate = $1/\text{time}/s^{-1}$ (4 dp)	reaction rate $\times 10^{-2}/s \times 10^2$ (2 dp)
3	120	0.0083	0.83
5	80	0.0125	1.25
7	40	0.0250	2.5
9	90	0.0111	1.11
11	140	0.0071	0.71

Much easier to plot

Same results

D. % change

Any conclusion you draw will be enhanced if you can quote a % change. This is Year 8 arithmetic so should not frighten off a sixth form student.

Calculate it like this:

$$\% \text{ increase} = \frac{\text{actual increase}}{\text{initial value}} \times 100\% = \frac{\text{final value} - \text{initial value}}{\text{initial value}} \times 100\%$$

E. Q_{10}

If you investigate the effect of temperature on the rate of an enzyme-controlled reaction, you will get results that allow you to plot a graph like that shown on page 26. One way of assessing your accuracy is to calculate Q_{10} from your graph, because theory tells us it should equal about 2. The closer your calculated value is to 2, the more accurate it is.

Grade boost

It is useful to quote a % change in the conclusion of the experiment you write up for BY3 or BY6.

Pointer

The closer your calculated value of Q_{10} is to 2, the more accurate your experiment has been.

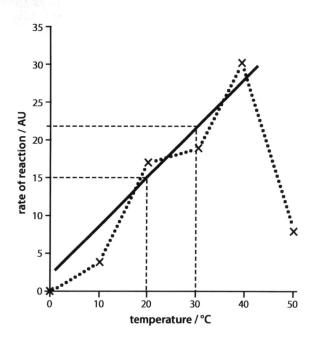

Draw a line of best fit using only the points where the rate is increasing.

Then read the rate of reaction at two temperatures that are 10°C apart.

On the graph
rate at 30°C = 22 AU
and rate at 20°C = 15 AU

$$Q_{10} = \frac{\text{rate at } (t + 10)°C}{\text{rate at } t°C} = \frac{22}{15} = 1.46 \text{ (2 dp)}$$

That means that the set of results that produced this graph is not very accurate, but yours might be better. It doesn't matter as long as you can discuss the sources of error and how you might improve the experiment.

F. R_f

When you learn about photosynthesis at A2, you may separate photosynthetic pigments by chromatography. You will end up with a plate or paper strip with pigment spots at various distances from the origin. Each pigment travels a characteristic proportion of the total distance moved by the solvent. If you work out this proportion, called R_f, you can identify each pigment.

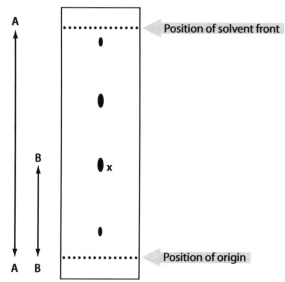

For the pigment spot labelled x, $R_f = \dfrac{\text{distance moved by x}}{\text{distance moved by solvent front}}$

You can measure the distances with a ruler and calculate R_f for each spot and identify them all.

How to design a field work experiment

1. Why do field work?

When biologists talk about field work, they are referring to looking at plants and animals growing in the wild, not in a lab. In a lab, you can control environmental factors like temperature and light intensity, but in the wild, you can't. So field work is a way of looking at plants and animals in their natural environment and seeing how they behave in the real world.

Not only can you design experiments to ask questions about how individuals behave, but also about how groups of individuals, whole populations of one species or communities of many species behave. You could test the effects of physical factors, such as the effect of soil pH on heather population density, or the effect of water depth on water shrimp population. You could test chemical factors in the environment, such as the effect of nitrate concentration on the number of bloodworms in a stream.

Field work techniques are powerful ways of monitoring populations and the effects on them.

At A Level, you are not required to do specific field work exercises but if you do, you will understand parts of BY4 and BY5 much better. You will also have a wonderful time.

2. Designing field work experiments

The same principles apply to field work as to lab-based experiments so you have to consider variables, accuracy and reliability in the same way. But there are particular issues you have to think about because, unlike in a lab, you cannot control significant environmental factors. And because organisms show variation, to understand properly what your results mean, you have to interrogate the data with statistical tests. One thing at a time.

A. Variables

Your field work experiment will test the effect of an environmental factor, the independent variable, on something biological, the dependent variable. Here are some examples:

Independent variable	Dependent variable
Light intensity	Area of bramble leaves
	Length of soft rush leaves
Soil compaction	% cover of plantain
Distance from drainage outlet into a stream	Number of bloodworms
Water depth in a stream	Number of water shrimp
Water flow rate in a stream	Number of mayfly larvae
Outcrop aspect	Species diversity of lichens
Soil water content	% cover of moss

>> *Pointer*

In these days of climate change, pollution and soil degradation, we will need more ecologists to find out what is happening and publicise the threats to species, populations, communities and their habitats. This could be you.

B. Controlled variables

As in a lab experiment, you want only the independent variable to change, but in the field you cannot control the environment. So you have to choose the sites for your experiment which are as similar as possible in every way other than the independent variable. Then you would have to monitor the most important factors, to ensure that they stay similar enough not to make a significant difference to your dependent variable.

Example 1

If you are doing an experiment with plants, among the most important factors in their growth are the light intensity and air temperature. So if you were investigating the effect of mowing on the species diversity of plants, you would choose a long grass area and a short grass area but do your best to ensure that they have the same light intensity, by making sure that the tree cover was similar and that they have the same air temperature by doing the whole experiment in as short a time as possible.

Example 2

If you are doing an experiment with aquatic invertebrates, such as the effect of nitrate concentration on leech numbers, you would only sample in areas that had similar water depths and flow rates.

C. Sampling

i)   If your experiment is along an environmental gradient, you would use a transect. This is a line along which you sample. The further you go along the line, the further along the gradient you are.

Example

Investigating the density of limpets at increasing height above sea level. The further along the transect you go, the higher above sea level you are. You would sample by placing a quadrat at regular intervals along the line and count how many limpets in each.

The actual length of your transect depends on where you are. It needs to be long enough to cover enough of the gradient to give you a meaningful result. But if it is too long, at the ends, there won't be any change, and so there is no need to take results there. It needs to be just long enough to cover the whole change.

ii) If there were no environmental gradient, but a uniform environment, in theory you would count every shrimp in the river or measure every ground ivy leaf in the field. Obviously you can't, so you have to sample. You are after enough organisms to get a reliable mean and they have to be representative of the whole population.

The way to do it is called block sampling. You set up two axes, at right angles and use random coordinates at which to sample. Let's say you want 15 samples. Go up to the first 15 people you see and ask them for the last two digits in their phone number. Here are your coordinates. The first of the digits is your x coordinate and the second is the y coordinate.

If you are placing a quadrat at each coordinate, always put the same corner of the quadrat on the coordinate. People usually use the bottom left-hand corner, as shown in the diagram. This is a way of being consistent and enhances your overall accuracy.

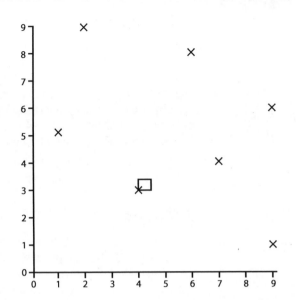

How many quadrats?

You can decide beforehand how many quadrats to do. But if you are not sure, you could calculate a running mean. This means that you calculate a new mean every time you do a quadrat reading. When the mean is the same for two quadrats in a row, you have enough. Do just one more.

Type of quadrat

i) If you are looking at the distribution of the alga *Pleurococcus* on tree trunks, it is best to use a grid printed on to acetate, which you can bend around the trunk and see through.

ii) If you are investigating water beetles in a 5m wide stream, a solid, open frame quadrat is best.

iii) If you are investigating % frequency of plants along a transect, you could use a 0.5m point frame quadrat.

iv) If you are assessing % cover, a gridded quadrat is best.

But what size quadrat?

Often, you have no choice, because the standard 0.5m × 0.5m is all that is available. You can work out the best size by a preliminary experiment. Start with a small quadrat and make the counts. Then double the area and repeat the counts. Keep doubling the area and repeating the counts until doubling the area does not increase the number you count. Then you have found the optimum area of quadrat.

D. Control experiment

You can't do a control experiment in the sense that you inactivate the independent variable. However, just as in a control experiment in the lab, you must keep all the variables constant, other than the independent variable that you have chosen. This is not always possible because, in fact, you cannot control the conditions in the field. So you choose your sampling areas to be as similar as possible, with the exception of the independent variable.

Grade boost

Using this way of checking the number of quadrats would be a useful improvement to write about in the analysis of your experiment.

Grade boost

Using this way of checking the right size quadrat would be a useful improvement to write about in the analysis of your experiment.

Grade boost

The least accurate part of a field experiment is usually to do with assessing the dependent variable, i.e. the biotic factor. It's worth explaining that in your write up.

E. Reliability

As with lab experiments, you have to take multiple readings and calculate a mean. Each quadrat position gives you a reading and with block sampling, all you do is average the 15 you have taken. But along a transect you only have one point at each distance. You could put the quadrat either side of the line to give two readings at each distance and calculate a mean of those or, depending on the situation, you could lay three transects parallel with each other and close by. Then you take results at the same distances along each. These are the replicates.

If you are testing a correlation, repeat readings are not possible. You must take enough readings to make your statistical test valid. This is discussed on page 31.

F. Accuracy

In your experiment, you will be measuring the effect of an abiotic factor on animals or plants. The measurements of the abiotic factors, such as concentration of dissolved oxygen in the stream, soil temperature or light intensity in the field are likely to be accurate because you will use properly calibrated equipment. It is the biotic data which limits the accuracy of the experiment overall and this will vary enormously, depending on your experiment. You may be counting numbers of larvae and some may be hidden in weeds, making it impossible to see them. Or you may be identifying plants, and without considerable experience, they can be misidentified. So you do the best you can and admit the problems. You can shake the weeds in a water sample and get out as many larvae as you can. You can take a field guide to help you identify plants.

G. Risk assessment

The major hazards in field work are very different from those in the lab. Whatever habitat you are in, sunburn is a hazard. In a terrestrial habitat, bites and stings are hazards, especially if you have particular allergies. Slips and trips and falling branches also have to be considered. If you are working in an aquatic habitat, Weil's disease, caused by the bacterium *Leptospira*, must be avoided and so you cover all cuts and wear rubber gloves or surgical gloves to protect yourself. Drowning is best avoided.

3. Graphs

The type of graph you draw will depend on the experiment you have done. There are four common ways of displaying field work data:

- **Line graph** – if you are investigating the number of bloodworms at different distances from a sewage outlet into a stream.
- **Scatter graph** – if you are testing the effect of light intensity on the width of ground ivy leaves.
- **Bar charts** – these are useful if you are comparing two habitats and have calculated the mean value of your biotic factor for each, e.g. if you have investigated the % cover of lichen on north and south facing rocks.
- **Kite diagrams** – these are used if you are looking at the changing distribution of plants along a transect. They show the changes very clearly.

4. Analysis of field work data

Sometimes the aim of your experiment is easily answered:

Example

Aim: to test the effect of nitrate ion concentration on the number of mayfly nymphs in a stream.

You would clearly see that the number of mayfly nymphs decreases as the nitrate ion concentration increases. This is because the increase in nitrate concentration is correlated with a decrease in concentration of dissolved oxygen. Mayfly nymphs have a high dependence on dissolved oxygen and their numbers fall significantly as the oxygen concentration decreases.

For an experiment like this, you could show your results with a graph like this:

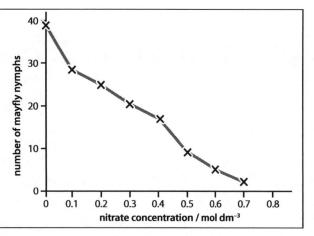

A statistical test could be used to test if there is a correlation, but if your results are very clear, at A Level, you might choose not to. When you become a politically aware ecologist, however, statistics would be essential evidence for your cause.

Sometimes the data do not give you such a clear result and then you would have to use statistics to test the meaning of your results. You must state a null hypothesis, as this hypothesis is what you are testing.

Example

Aim: to test if there is a difference in the height:width ratio of periwinkles on rocky shores with high or low exposure.

Null hypothesis: there is no difference in the height:width ratio of periwinkles on rocky shores with high or low exposure.

Your experiment and statistics test if the null hypothesis can be rejected. It is a philosophical matter to seek to reject the null hypothesis, rather than accept it, because it is easier in experimental work to show a suggestion is untrue than to show that it is true.

Which test?

There are three tests that are especially useful in this sort of work and it is easy to decide which to use. Decide before you start the experiment which you expect to use. This may have a bearing on the number of readings you make.

1. Use the t-test if you are comparing the means of the two sets of data. Three requirements make this test valid:

   - Each set of data is normally distributed – plot a frequency histogram to see. An approximately normal distribution means you can use this test.
   AND
   - you have at least 15 samples in each data set
   AND
   - you are using raw data, not manipulated data.

>> **Pointer**

The null hypothesis states that the independent variable has no effect on the dependent variable. You must always give a null hypothesis at the start of a statistical test.

Grade boost

Note the terminology – statistics do not prove or disprove. It tests a null hypothesis and then either rejects or accepts it.

>> **Pointer**

There are three common statistical tests for field work. Make sure you choose the right one: student's t-test, Mann–Whitney U-test, Spearman Rank Correlation test.

≫ Pointer
Please don't call it the
Mann-U Whitney test.

2. Use the Mann–Whitney U-test to compare two medians. You can use this test if:
   - the data is not normally distributed, which you can tell from the frequency histogram

   OR

   - you have fewer than 15 samples in each data set

   OR

   - the data is manipulated.

3. Use the Spearman Rank Correlation test if you are looking for a correlation:

   > **Example**
   >
   > **Aim:** to test the effect of light intensity on the % cover of meadow grass.
   >
   > **Null hypothesis:** there is no correlation between the height of meadow grass and the light intensity at which it grows.

   Make sure you have at least 15 sets of results. If you plot a graph of your results, you do not need to add line of best fit. The statistics will tell you if a line is justified or not.

Experiment design checklist

Design area	Detail	I have done this
Aim	Clearly state aim in terms of two variables	
Prediction	Describe what you think will happen	
Independent variable	Clear statement	
	Five values	
Dependent variable	Clear statement	
	Units	
Controlled variables	Decide the two most important and name them	
	Values for each, with units	
Repeats	State how many	
Control experiment	Identify which feature is inactivated	
	Identify what stays the same	
	If there is no suitable control know why not and what control is for	
Hazard	Identify hazard	
	Know what the risk is	
	Know how to minimise risk	
	Know what to do if hazard occurs	
Construct results table	Detailed column headings	
	Units in column headings only	
	Enough repeats or an explanation as to why not	
	Appropriate data recording to suitable number of decimal places	

3: Standard experiments

This section will introduce you to some standard experiments and give examples of how to approach their design. You may do similar experiments and so you can adapt this information to suit what you are doing in the lab or in the field.

Enzyme experiments

Aim	Independent variable	Dependent variable	Method summary	Controlled variables Variable	Controlled variables Value	Control
To show the effect of temperature on rate of reaction of amylase digesting starch	Temperature, e.g. 20°C, 40°C, 60°C, 80°C, 100°C	Rate of digestion = 1/time taken for complete starch digestion / min⁻¹ or s⁻¹	Time incubation period required for all the starch to be digested so that iodine solution does not turn black when added	Enzyme concentration; Starch concentration	0.1g/100cm³; 1.0g/100cm³	Boil the amylase for 10 minutes and cool it for the experiment at each temperature
To show the effect of pH on the volume of oxygen produced when catalase digests hydrogen peroxide	pH, e.g. 2, 4, 6, 8, 10	Volume of oxygen produced in 5 minutes/cm³	Put potato discs in different pH buffers. Measure oxygen volume produced by their catalase 5 minutes after the addition of hydrogen peroxide	Concentration of catalase by having the same number of potato discs; Hydrogen peroxide concentration	30 discs; 20 vol	Boil the potato discs in water for 10 minutes and cool before using at each pH
To show the effect of casein concentration on the rate at which trypsin digests it	Casein concentration provided by different concentrations of milk powder, e.g. 0, 1, 2, 3, 4 g/100cm³	Rate of digestion = 1/time for milk to change from white to clear / min⁻¹ or s⁻¹	Time how long each mixture of milk and trypsin takes to clear	Temperature; Trypsin concentration	30°C; 0.5 g/100cm³	Boil the trypsin for 10 minutes and cool then use it at each concentration
To show the effect of lactase concentration on the rate of lactose digestion using immobilised lactase	Lactase concentration, given by different number of immobilised lactase balls, e.g. 0, 20, 40, 60, 80 balls	Concentration of glucose produced /mol dm⁻³	Incubate same volume of milk over different numbers of lactase balls for same time. Use glucose-measuring strips to measure glucose concentration in product	Temperature; Milk concentration	25°C; 4g/100cm³ milk powder	Boil the lactase for 10 minutes and cool before making balls; perform the experiment at each ball number

Photosynthesis experiments

Aim	Independent variable	Dependent variable	Method summary	Controlled variables Variable	Value	Control
To compare R_f values for pigments in spinach leaves	Pigment type, e.g. chlorophyll a and b, carotene, xanthophyll	R_f = distance moved by pigment/distance moved by solvent front	Separate spinach pigments by paper chromatography with propanol/petroleum ether solvent	Temperature; Propanol:pet ether ratio	25°C; 4:1	n/a
To determine the effect of light intensity on the rate of photosynthesis given by different distances of light source	Light intensity given by different distances of light source, e.g. 0.2, 0.4, 0.6, 0.8, 1.0m	Time for hydrogen carbonate indicator to turn from red to yellow/min or s	Suspend algae, e.g. *Scenedesmus* in alginate balls and incubate in hydrogen carbonate indicator at various distances from light source. Time the indicator's colour change from red to yellow	Temperature; Carbon dioxide concentration	25°C; 0.05 mol dm^{-3} NaHCO$_3$	Boil algal suspension for 10 minutes and cool before making alginate balls

Transpiration experiments

Aim	Independent variable	Dependent variable	Method summary	Controlled variables Variable	Value	Control
To determine the effect of light intensity on the rate of transpiration	Light intensity given by light distance from shoot source, e.g. 0.2, 0.4, 0.6, 0.8, 1.0m	Transpiration rate, measured by the distance travelled by a meniscus along a capillary tube/mm	Set up potometer and take readings of meniscus movement with light source at different distances along a metre rule. Equilibrate shoot for 5 minutes with lamp at each distance before making readings	Air movement; Air humidity	Still air; Ambient humidity	Repeat experiment with all leaves removed
To determine the effect of air movement on the rate of transpiration	Air movement given by settings on a cold air hair dryer, e.g. 0, 1, 2, 3, 4	Transpiration rate, measured by the distance travelled by a meniscus along a capillary tube/mm	Set up potometer and take readings of meniscus movement with hair dryer at different settings. Equilibrate shoot for 5 minutes at each setting before making readings	Light intensity; Air humidity	Ambient light; Ambient humidity	Repeat experiment with all leaves removed

Respiration experiments

Aim	Independent variable	Dependent variable	Method summary	Controlled variables — Variable	Value	Control
To determine the effect of temperature on the rate of locust respiration	Temperature locust maintained at, e.g. 15°C, 25°C, 35°C, 45°C, 55°C	Rate of respiration as shown by abdominal movements, e.g. number of abdominal movements/minute	Locust in respirometer allowed to equilibrate to temperature for 5 minutes / Number of abdominal movements in 3 minutes counted to calculate mean/minute	Light intensity / Volume available	Ambient / Kept in same boiling tube for each reading	n/a
To determine the effect of temperature on the rate of respiration of yeast	Temperature at which yeast maintained, e.g. 20°C, 35°C, 50°C, 65°C, 80°C	Time taken for methylene blue to turn colourless/minutes	Yeast and sucrose solution equilibrated separately to temperature and mixed with methylene blue; maintained at given temperature and timed for disappearance of blue colour	Concentration of yeast suspension / Volume of methylene blue	$10g/100cm^3$ suspension / $0.1cm^3$	Yeast suspension boiled for 10 minutes and cooled before using at each temperature

Field work experiments

Aim	Independent variable	Dependent variable	Method summary	Controlled variables — Variable	Value	Control
To determine the effect of light intensity on the % cover of ground ivy along a transect	Light intensity given by distance along transect from a wooded area into a field	% cover ground ivy	Set up 5m transect from a wooded area into a field / At 1m intervals assess % cover of ground ivy in a 0.5m × 0.5m open quadrat	Air temperature / Ground humidity	20°C / 70%	n/a
To compare the effect of fast and slow water flow rate on the number of mayfly nymphs in a stream	Water flow rate – still water or approximately $2m\,s^{-1}$	Number of mayfly nymphs	Find 10 sites in still water and 10 sites on water flowing at approximately the same speed and place 0.5m × 0.5m open frame quadrat on stream bed / Kick sample for 2 minutes and count mayfly nymphs retrieved in net after 30 seconds	Water temperature / Water depth	16°C / 0.1m	n/a

4: Writing up your BY3 or BY6 experiment for assessment

Using the booklet

Cover – when you write up your BY3 or BY6 practical assessment you will have a booklet to write in. Standard information goes on the front, like your name and candidate number. It is surprising how many candidates put the wrong number. You don't lose marks for it, but it looks better to get it right.

Title – you will need a brief title. This is just to give your examiner an idea of what to expect. Use the aim to guide you.

> **Example**
>
> **Aim:** To investigate the effect of soil moisture content on the length of bramble internodes.
>
> **Title:** An investigation into the effect of soil moisture content on the length of bramble internodes.

Signatures – don't forget to sign. Your teacher will also have to sign and date the booklet to acknowledge that you have completed the work in accordance with all the requirements. Be aware that sometimes teachers choose not to sign, which indicates that the experiment was not carried out or written up in a manner that the teacher thought suitable. So do not try to bend rules. Apart from it being morally wrong, you risk losing a mark if you do.

Prompts – inside the front cover of the booklet is the list of areas to cover in your write up. Here it is:

> You should write the report of your investigation using the following headings in sequence.
>
> 1. Aim/Prediction
> 2. Experimental design
>   Details of Independent variable – range; units
>   Details of Dependent variable – units
>   Details of Controlled variables – values
>   Repeatability
>   Control experiment
>   Safety risk assessment
> 3. Results
>   Suitable table
>   (Headings; units; repeats; recording)
>   Graph or statistical test as appropriate
>   (Axis labels; units; grid use; scales; plots; line)
> 4. Analysis of results
>   Trend
>   Consistency
>   Sources of uncertainty plus improvement
>   Explain/relate results to theory
>   Conclusion
> 5. Plan for further work
>   Further investigation with different independent variable
>   Controlled variables
>   Expected results

 Pointer
This list is all you are allowed to have with you when you write up, so make sure you have read very carefully about all these headings and thought about what they mean for your experiment.

Use these headings in the order given. They are there to prompt you. If you write about each and then leave a line before moving on to the next, your thoughts will be organised and each page will look organised too. You could write each sub-heading to help you focus your thoughts. For each paragraph, as you write, ask yourself, 'Is what I am writing now directly related to the subheading?' and if the answer is 'No', think again.

Graph – at the back of the booklet is graph paper and your examiner will find it. But if you have done a field work experiment for BY6 and you have included statistics, the examiner will mark either the graph or the stats, whichever they come to first.

Rough work – there's room in the booklet for your rough work. You may, for example, like to do your table in rough first, then copy it neatly when you write up the experiment. Some people like to make notes about each section before beginning the formal report.

Pointer

If you want the graph and not the stats to be assessed, make that very clear by writing 'Please mark graph not stats' or something similar, and vice versa.

Grade boost

Remember to cross the rough work through with a single line when it is finished. Your examiner will look at it. It has been known for candidates to forget to write something in the formal write up but get credit for it anyway because it was mentioned in the rough work. So leave it legible.

Explanation of marking criteria

The criteria for BY3 and BY6 are very similar and the booklet prompts apply to both. Here is an explanation of the prompts.

Pointer

The information given here will be useful to you if you study either Biology or Human Biology because the same principles apply.

1. Aim / Prediction

You must say what your experiment is designed to find out and identify the independent and dependent variables. You must also describe the effect you expect to see.

independent variable   *dependent variable*

Example

Aim: To investigate the effect of potato disc number on the volume of oxygen produced by catalase in hydrogen peroxide breakdown.

Prediction: As the number of potato discs increases, the oxygen volume will increase.

---

prediction links the two variables with the direction of the effect

If you are writing about an enzyme experiment, it is important to name both the enzyme and the substrate in the aim, rather than just saying 'enzyme' or 'substrate'. For example, you should write:

Aim: to test the effect of trypsin concentration in the rate of digestion of milk protein.

NOT Aim: to test the effect of enzyme concentration in the rate of digestion of substrate.

Make sure that you write about what is actually plotted on the graph. Many people predict a change in rate but then go on to plot time instead. It doesn't matter which you do but you must be consistent.

Pointer

Keep the aim simple. Just test one thing. Multiple aims will not produce more marks and they make the experiment too complex.

2. Experimental design

A. Independent variable

Even though you have already stated your aim, you must say, explicitly, 'The independent variable is ...' and then you must give a minimum of five values for it. Say what they are because your examiner will not go hunting for them in your graph or results table. In many cases, one of the values could be zero, but include it anyway.

> **Example**
>
> **Aim:** to test the effect of lead nitrate concentration on the length of mung bean radicles four days after germination.
>
> **The independent variable** is the concentration of lead nitrate.
>
> Its values will be 0, 0.05, 0.10, 0.15 and 0.20 mol dm^{-3}.

5 values   don't forget the units

Practical tip

The units of concentration of hydrogen peroxide are 'vol'.

NB 1: if you are using hydrogen peroxide, its concentration is measured in units called 'vol'. That's because it decomposes to give oxygen and the more hydrogen peroxide you have in solution, the bigger the volume of oxygen that is made:

1 dm^3 1 vol hydrogen peroxide gives 1 dm^3 oxygen

1 dm^3 2 vol hydrogen peroxide gives 2 dm^3 oxygen

Practical tip

If you use % as a concentration, make it clear what % means. Is it g/100cm^3 or is it a dilution of a stock solution?

NB 2: using the unit % when describing a solution has a problem because it can mean two different things. If you are diluting a stock solution to get different concentrations for your independent variable, make it clear that a 10% solution is 10% of a stock solution. The confusion arises because 10% could also mean 10g per 100cm^3 solution. Be very clear which you mean.

NB 3 Field work:

i) if you are comparing two habitats, obviously you can't give five values for the independent variable. Say what the two habitats are and give approximate values if relevant.

> **Aim:** to compare the leech numbers in still and flowing water.
>
> **The independent variable** is the water movement and is either zero (in still water) or approximately 1 m s^{-1} in the stream.

ii) the only time you are justified in using the word 'amount' is if you are considering the amount of trampling.

> **Aim:** to test the effect of the amount of trampling on the % cover of the grass Yorkshire fog.

Grade boost

Only use the word 'amount' when you are testing the effects of soil trampling.

B. Dependent variable

This is what you will be measuring, counting or calculating. It will already have appeared in your aim and this is what you will plot on the *y* axis of your graph and discuss in your analysis. You must say what units you will use for it.

Example

Aim: to investigate the effect of trypsin concentration on the time taken to digest the casein in milk.

The dependent variable is the time taken to digest the casein, in other words, the time taken for the milk to change from white to clear. It will be measured in seconds.

But if the aim referred to the rate of reaction, not the time, then the dependent variable would be rate and would be measured in sec^{-1}, because you would calculate it using the formula rate = 1/time. In this case, the graph would have rate of reaction plotted on the *y* axis and the discussion would all be about rate, not about time. Do not discuss both and do not keep changing which you are writing about. You will lose a mark if you are not completely consistent.

In a field work experiment, you might be calculating a biotic index as your dependent variable. The commonest are Disney's, Simpson's and the Lincoln index. There are no units for these because they are arithmetical devices using counts, so you would need to explain that.

C. Controlled variables

You only need to give two controlled variables, but they must be the most important two. You must also give their values.

Example 1

Aim: to test the effect of pH on the time taken for amylase to digest of starch.

Controlled variables:

The amylase concentration will be kept constant at 0.1%, i.e. 0.1g per 100cm³ amylase solution.

The concentration of casein will be kept constant by using solutions containing 4% milk powder, i.e. 4g milk powder per 100cm³ of solution.

In the example above, two important factors are given as the controlled variables. Of course there are others that could be used, such as the volume of amylase, the volume of milk and the temperature.

Example 2

Aim: to test the effect of urea concentration on the time taken for urease to digest urea.

You must give a suitable value but it is not always pH7. If you use pepsin, a suitable pH is 2.

Controlled variables:

1. pH will be kept constant at pH7 by using a pH7 buffer.
2. the temperature at which reaction is carried out will be 30°C, using an electronically controlled water bath.

It is not enough just to say the pH will be kept constant.

≫ *Pointer*

Remind yourself whether you are writing about time or rate. It doesn't matter which but you must be consistent in the aim, prediction, results, graph, analysis and conclusion.

⏏ Grade boost

One mark for two controlled variables.
Second mark for their values.
One controlled variable + one value – no marks.

•••Practical tip•••

Many experiments have temperature as a controlled variable. You use the thermometer to measure the temperature, not to keep it constant.

Do not say that the temperature will be kept constant by using room temperature. This is much too vague, and in any case, room temperature changes. Always state a particular temperature. If you are using human enzymes, 37°C is a suitable temperature, but plant and fungal enzymes may have completely different optimum temperatures and so 37°C would not be suitable for them.

If you are doing field work, you must explain that it is not possible to control the environment, so you would choose sites where the environmental factors are as similar as you can get them. You would then measure them to be sure that, while unlikely to be identical as they would be in a lab experiment, they are close enough to have no significant effect on the dependent variable.

Field work example

Aim: to test the effect of soil pH on the density of dog's mercury.

Light intensity and air temperature are significant factors in controlling plant growth so it would be sensible to have those as the controlled variables. You would set up a 10m × 10m sampling area and place 15 quadrats at random coordinates for counting dog's mercury. To monitor the dependent variables, at each quadrat you would measure light intensity and air temperature. The readings in each quadrat should be similar.

D. Repeatability

In your design, you need to state that you are making three readings for each value of your independent variable. In fact, the more readings you take, the more reliable the mean is, but at this level, and given the time you have available, three is appropriate.

You need to explain why you are making the repeats and explain that it diminishes the uncertainty in your measurements and increases the confidence you have in drawing conclusions from the data. If all your readings are close, then your results show repeatability. The spread around the mean is a measure of the repeatability and is another way of describing reliability. It will be shown on the graph by the range bars or, for some field work experiments, the standard deviation bars you draw.

In field work experiments it is not possible to make exact replicate readings. You can never step into the same river twice. You should explain this to your examiner, and explain that your reliability is enhanced by representative sampling, and the number of readings taken is accounted for in the statistical test.

E. Control experiment

There are two marks available for describing the control experiment and even if you have not done one, you can still get these two marks. If you have done a control, say what it is:

Example 1

Aim: to test the effect of pH on the time taken for pepsin to digest egg white.

Control experiment: the pepsin solution was boiled for 10 minutes to denature the enzyme and then it was cooled before use.

NB don't forget to write that you cool the enzyme before using it.

In Example 1, the active agent in the experiment, i.e. the enzyme, was removed and so no digestion is expected, showing that the pepsin is responsible for the digestion. You must also say that to show that it is the pepsin that is responsible, all other conditions must stay the same, i.e. egg white volume and concentration, pepsin volume, temperature, pH of solution. You could just say 'all other conditions remain the same' but specifying them produces a more thorough write up.

Grade boost

Remember to comment that the more readings you take, the more reliable the mean is.

Pointer

If you are making counts in a quadrat, you can work out when you have done enough readings. You recalculate the mean with every additional result. This is called a running mean and you will know when you have enough readings because the running mean will stop changing as you take more results.

Example 2

Aim: to test the effect of light source distance on the volume of oxygen emitted by algae suspended in alginate balls.

Control experiment: the algal suspension was boiled for 10 minutes to kill the algae. They were cooled before being suspended in alginate balls.

Example 2 shows that the algae are responsible for the changing volumes of oxygen evolved.

As explained on page 22 a control is not a zero value of the independent variable, e.g. distilled water instead of enzyme or no light in a photosynthesis experiment. The control must specifically remove the active ingredient.

In some experiments, there is no control because there is no active ingredient to remove. This is often the case when you are making a direct comparison:

Example 3

Aim: to determine the species diversity in long grass and short grass areas.

Example 3 has no suitable control because removing the grass has no meaning in this experiment. If this were your experiment, you must explain why no control is possible and that would get you a mark. You would then discuss what a control is used for and be awarded the second mark.

F. Risk assessment

There are three things you have to write about in the context of the risk assessment. You must identify the hazard, say why it is a hazard and say what you would do to minimise the risk. Sometimes, students do not know the difference between a hazard and a risk. The hazard is the item that might cause you harm, e.g. the rusty scalpel blade or the ethanol next to a flame. The risk is what could happen, e.g. septicaemia from the blade; burns from the fire.

You must identify the most significant hazard in your experiment, so do not write about tying back your hair, wearing a lab coat, putting your bag under the bench or not running in the lab. This is altogether far too Year 7.

Here is a list of types of experiment and the hazards they present. As you also have to explain how you will minimise harm, suggestions for this are put in the third column. Your experiment may be about something else entirely and you will have to consider its risks.

 Grade boost

Don't forget to mention that after you boil an enzyme or algae for the control experiment you have to cool them before use.

Experiment type	Major hazard	Hazard control
Enzymes	Allergic reaction of skin in response to foreign protein	Avoid skin contact and wash with soap and water if contact occurs
	Proximity of water and electricity	Place water bath at distance from electric socket; take care not to splash water; immediately mop up any spilt liquid
Catalase	Cutting potato discs with sharp scalpel	Care with dissecting equipment; if skin cut or pierced, wash with soap and water immediately
	Hydrogen peroxide is an irritant	Avoid skin contact and wear goggles
Photosynthesis	Burn from hot lamp	Avoid skin contact with bulb; 10 minutes in cold water if burned
	Eye damage from halogen light source	Avoid looking directly into lamp
Bacterial cultures	Infection with pathogens	Use sterile technique; do not open dishes once set up; incubate culture below 30°C; autoclave dishes prior to disposal to kill bacteria
Field work at coast	Slipping on rocks	Wear suitable shoes; walk very carefully; work within earshot of others in case of accident
	Getting cut off by tide coming in	Check tide tables before beginning work; work within earshot of others
Field work using bodies of water	Drowning	Walk very carefully; work within earshot of others in case of accident
	Weil's disease	Use rubber gloves to avoid contact with water; keep cuts covered
Terrestrial field work	Tripping	Walk very carefully; work within earshot of others in case of accident
	Poisonous plants and animals	Avoid ingesting any biological material; wear appropriate clothing to keep skin covered
	Getting lost	Work within earshot of others; carry mobile phone with emergency contact numbers

>> *Pointer*

To protect your eyes, you wear goggles, not googles.

>> *Pointer*

'Hazard' has one z. With two it is an American TV programme from the early 1980s.

3. Results

Your results will be displayed in a table. If you construct your table before you take any readings, the results can be written directly into the table.

Column headings

The way you head the columns is crucial. The column headings must be complete and units must be included in the column headings:

> **Examples**
>
> 'time for methylene blue to turn colourless / s', not just 'time / s'
> or 'volume of oxygen produced in 5 minutes / cm³', not just 'volume / cm³'

Arranging the table

You will need a column for the independent variable and then four columns for the dependent variable. These four are three for the three readings and one for the mean:

Example

Aim: to test the effect of temperature on colony diameter of cultures of *Streptococcus albus*.

Results:

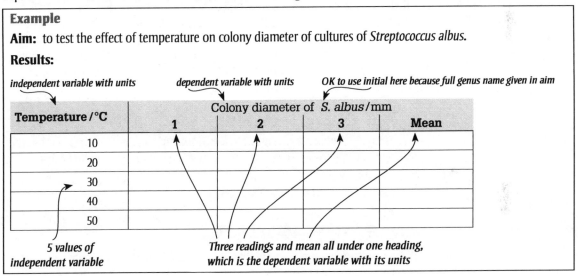

independent variable with units   *dependent variable with units*   *OK to use initial here because full genus name given in aim*

Temperature /°C	Colony diameter of *S. albus* /mm			
	1	2	3	Mean
10				
20				
30				
40				
50				

5 values of independent variable   *Three readings and mean all under one heading, which is the dependent variable with its units*

What type of average?

'Mean' is a better word than 'average'. If you write the word 'average', it will be assumed that you mean mean, but in fact, you might mean mode or median. So choose words with care. If it is was a mean that you calculated, write mean. Remember to include the mean column under the heading for the dependent variable, so its units are clearly shown.

Which units?

Take care when you write the units that they make sense. If you are giving a length, mm or metres are best as they are SI units. For volumes, cm³ or dm³ are the commonest and, being SI units, are preferable to ml and litres. If you have calculated an area, make sure the units are correct. It is too easy to write mm³ when you mean mm².

>> *Pointer*

Write units in the column headings only. Do not write them in the cells of the table. The cells have numbers only.

Grade boost

No units appear in the cells of the table as the cells are for numbers only. The convention these days is not to put the units in brackets, but to write an oblique after the heading and before the unit, as the example below shows.

>> *Pointer*

Some people prefer to put the mean in a different table because it is a calculated value rather than a reading. If you do, remember to head the independent variable column correctly and to include the heading for the dependent variable.

Units and decimal places

The most important thing is BE CONSISTENT. But also be sensible.

The thermometer may have calibrations one degree apart. All you write then is the number, e.g. 20°C, not 20.0°C. If you go to one decimal place, the implication is that you can read to $\pm 0.1°$.

You may use an electronic timer that gives the time to ± 0.01s. Sadly your reaction time is not this good so it is meaningless to give times to this degree of accuracy. Depending on the experiment, the nearest second may be suitable, e.g. if you are timing how long it takes to collect 10cm³ oxygen. But if you are timing how long it takes for methylene blue to decolorise, it is impossible to be that precise because the colour change is gradual. In this case, it may be better to read to the nearest minute. As the SI units of time are seconds, if you choose a different unit, such as minutes, explain underneath your table what you have done and why. It will not give you more marks, but it shows your examiner that you understand what you are doing and it makes a better report.

•• **Practical tip** ••

If you are recording time, stick to one unit only. Do not mix minutes and seconds.

Something to avoid

If you are recording time use one unit only. It may be seconds, it may be minutes but what it must not be is minutes and seconds. Sometimes people write 1.30 minutes. This probably means 1 minute 30 seconds but it may mean 1.30 minutes. Then when a mean is calculated, even if it meant 1 minute 30 seconds people treat it as 1.30 min and then their mean is wrongly calculated. All too confusing. Stick to one unit only. Do not mix.

Sometimes there are no units

If your experiment uses readings from a colorimeter, there are no units because the reading is a comparison. Then you must write AU or arbitrary units, and explain why.

If you are plotting a count then there will be no units. You would then label the axis 'number of ....' so it is clear that there are no units.

The mean and decimal places

When you calculate the mean, in theory you should use the same number of decimal places as in your readings, because a calculated value cannot be more accurate than the readings that produce it. But it is acceptable to use one more decimal place if it adds clarity. Once again, underneath the table, explain what you have done and why.

Except for the mean in some cases, the number of decimal places must be the same throughout the results table. You will lose a mark if it is not. Whether or not the mean has a different number of decimal places from the readings, make sure that within each vertical column, you always have a constant number of decimal places.

Repeats

Three is the best number. If for any reason, you have not done three, explain why underneath your table. In some cases, your teacher may provide you with another set of results to add to your own. Make sure it is very clear which are yours and which have been given to you.

4. Graph

How to get your seven marks:

1. **Axes:** Label both axes correctly and fully, just as in the column headings of
    the results table. The independent variable goes on the horizontal axis and the
    dependent variable goes on the vertical axis. If you are plotting means on the
    y axis, the label must say mean. It is truly alarming how many people forget to
    write 'mean' here.

    > **Example**
    >
    > **Aim:** to test the effect of alcohol concentration on the heart rate of *Daphnia*.
    >
    > With three readings at each alcohol concentration, you would calculate a mean
    > heart rate to plot. The vertical axis would be labelled 'mean heart rate of
    > *Daphnia* /beats per minute'.

    You don't need to write x or y on the axes and you don't need to put an arrow at
    the end of each.

2. **Scale:** Choose the scale carefully so that the data points that you plot will
    produce a line that covers at least half the available space on both axes.

Like this: **Not like this:**

 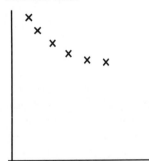

3. Make sure you have put the correct units on the axes. Check they are the same as
    in your table.

4. Choose scales that are easy to read. Choose scale divisions that divide by 5 or 10,
    not by three.

Like this: **Not like this:**

 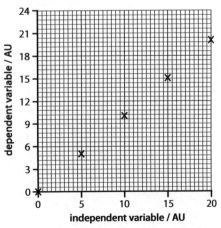

5. **Origin:** whether or not the scale starts at 0, there must be a number at the origin on both the *x* and the *y* axis.

Break lines can be used to make sure your data points cover a large part of the graph paper:

But you could avoid them by having the x axis start at 50°C:

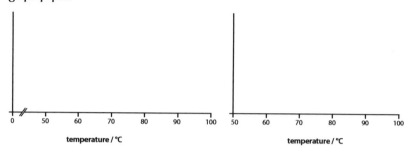

>>> *Pointer*

Do not start your scale, then use break lines and then continue with the scale. The break line comes immediately after a 0, or not at all.

6. **Points:** All the points must be plotted accurately. This is easier if you have chosen a sensible scale. Your examiner will check every point. If they are all correct, you get two marks.

One wrong loses you a mark and two wrong loses you both marks. It's worth taking the trouble to do it very accurately.

>>> *Pointer*

When you plot the points, make them visible. Dots disappear when you draw a line. Crosses are best with the centre of the cross at the exact coordinate.

7. **Lines:** Join the data points individually with a ruler, making sure you go from the centre of one cross to the centre of the next. Make sure you use a sharp HB pencil and that you rule it properly the first time and don't need to erase the line to try again. You will lose a mark if your line is not beautiful.

In Biology, it is the data points that are significant, so make sure the line does not obliterate them. The line is just a construct of your imagination. Unlike in Physics or Chemistry, we cannot assume a straight line relationship between the variables so a line of best fit is only occasionally justified. Because you only know what has happened in the range at which you measured, you are not justified in taking the line beyond the data points. So no extrapolation. This means that you cannot draw the line beyond the points at either end. Do not join the line to the origin unless there is a data point there.

 Grade boost

For the graph line, join point-to-point with a ruler. No extrapolation.

Like this:

Not like this:

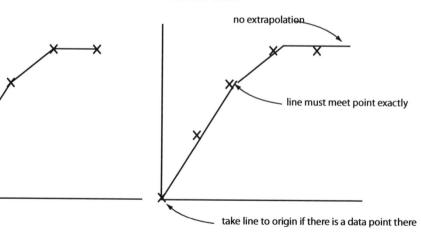

Experiment with line of best fit

If you are reading an intercept from the graph, a line of best fit is suitable. Make sure you explain why you have chosen a line of best fit, rather than joining the points.

Aim: to measure the water potential of potato cells.

You could measure the mass of potato chips before and after incubation in solutions of different water potentials. If you plot % mass change against water potential, the line will cross the x axis at the water potential of the cells. You can draw a line of best fit for this because the line will take into account the inaccuracy of each point so your intercept can be read more accurately than if you had taken only the two points either side.

The intercept shows that the water potential of the cells is −500 kPa.

Use of error bars

The commonest type of error bar at A Level is the range bar. You use this when each point on your graph is a mean value. You plot the highest and lowest readings for each, in addition to the mean. When you do this, draw a cross for your mean and two little bars for the highest and lowest readings.

Sometimes, people use crosses for all three and then the graph is much more difficult to interpret, so don't do that.

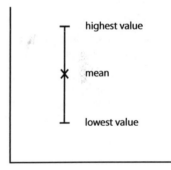

If you have done a field work experiment, it may be suitable to plot a bar chart showing two mean values and you can use you can use range bars here too:

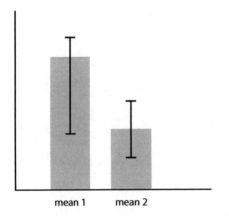

If you have done the sort of experiment that lets you plot a bar chart, you are likely to have done a t-test, in which case you will have calculated standard deviation. Instead of plotting range bars, you could plot standard deviation bars instead.

It doesn't matter which you do but remember to write somewhere on your graph 'bars show range' or 'bars show standard deviation'.

If you have done a field work experiment where you are testing a correlation, you would plot a scatter graph and so there will not be any error bars:

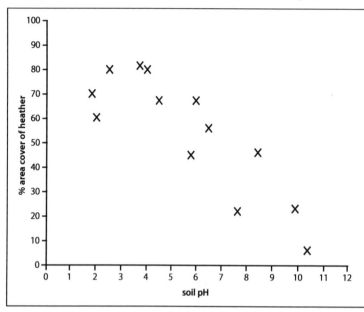

Example

Aim: to test the effect of soil pH on the % area cover of heather.

The scatter graph might look like this:

Although soil pH is the independent variable, you can only take results where you find them and as you are unlikely to find two patches of soil with exactly the same pH, there are no precise replicates.

So you cannot draw range bars.

It isn't appropriate to draw a line of best fit through these points because you cannot assume a straight line relationship. A statistical test will tell you if the assumption is justified.

5. Statistical analysis

If you do a field work experiment, you may analyse your data with a statistical test. Cynics say that you use statistics only when the answer isn't obvious. But that isn't true. You use statistics to analyse field data because genetic variation between organisms and the minute differences in abiotic factors prevent you from making true replicate readings. So without statistics, it would be hard to draw a valid conclusion.

Pointer

It is no harder to get the mark with statistics than it is with a graph.

Your examiner will mark your graph or your statistical test – whichever you prefer – but you must make it clear which you would like to have assessed. You could write after your results table 'Please mark graph' or 'Please mark statistics'. The examiner will like the word please. If you do not say which you want marked, the examiner will mark whichever is first.

When you present your statistical analysis, there are six things you have to do:

1. Explain why you have chosen this particular test – see pages 31–32.
2. State the null hypothesis.
3. Calculate the test statistic correctly. Your examiner will check.
4. Say how many degrees of freedom you are working to or explain that you are using a probability of 0.05 or that you are using 95% confidence limits.
5. Quote the critical value of the test statistic from the tables and say whether your calculated value is higher or lower.
6. Say whether you accept or reject the null hypothesis at the 0.05 level of significance.

6. Analysis

This is a big section of the write up and many students fail to get all the marks here because they do not clearly address the areas required. They are all written in the prompt sheet so take each one in turn and write about it as clearly as you can. The prompts are described here in order.

1. Trend

Describe what your graph tells you. First of all describe the general trend and say if it appears to be a direct relationship, i.e. straight line with a positive gradient, and say if it seems to go through the origin (Example 1). Or say if it is an inverse relationship, i.e. a straight line with negative gradient (Example 2). If the gradient seems to change, describe that (Example 3).

Example 1

Aim: to investigate the effect of enzyme concentration on the rate of reaction of amylase.

Trend: as the enzyme concentration increases, the rate of reaction increases. There is a positive gradient and the line goes through the origin.

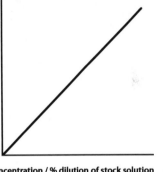

Example 2

Aim: to test the effect of soil compaction on the % cover of meadow grass.

Trend: as the soil compaction increases the % cover of meadow grass decreases. There appears to be an inverse relationship between the two.

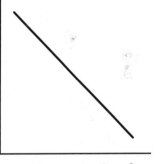

Example 3

Aim: to test the effect of temperature on the permeability of beetroot membranes.

Trend: there is a gradual increase in membrane permeability as the temperature increases up to 30°C. Above 30°C the gradient of the line increase sharply showing that permeability increases greatly so 30°C can be recognised as the transition temperature for this membrane.

For a field work experiment, you could state the conclusion derived from your statistical test:

Null hypothesis: there is no difference in the length of the water shrimp body in deep and shallow bodies of water.

Trend: the calculated value of t is greater than the critical value of t at 38 degrees of freedom and 0.05 probability, so the null hypothesis is rejected at the 0.05 level of significance.

Grade boost

You will not lose marks for unexpected results, as long as you describe them accurately and try to explain why you got them.

The trend you describe must refer to your own results and not what you expected to happen. Refer to your graph or table while describing the trend so that you examiner knows that you are thinking about what you actually found, rather than what the textbook says.

Word of warning: if your graph has a peak, only describe it as an optimum if you mean it is the best:

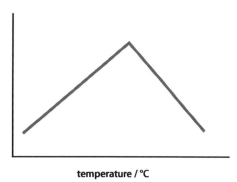

temperature / °C

An experiment to test the effect of temperature on enzyme activity might produce a graph with a peak. If that peak occurred at 45°C, you could say that the enzyme has an optimum temperature of 45°C.

But an experiment testing the effect of temperature on the number of aphids living on a bean plant might give you the same shape graph. You would not describe the temperature giving the highest number the optimum, because aphids destroy bean plants so there is nothing 'optimum' about the temperature that gives the highest number.

2. Consistency

Here you look at your raw results and see how similar the replicates at each value of the independent variable are. This is also described as reliability or repeatability:

Example

Aim: to assess the effect of water potential of a bathing solution on the % of cells that are plasmolysed.

In this experiment, you would float rhubarb epidermis in sucrose solutions with different water potentials for 30 minutes and then mount them on a microscope slide in a drop of that solution. Using your microscope, you could look at 100 cells and count how many of them are plasmolysed. You would make three separate slides at each water potential and these are the replicates.

Water potential of sucrose solution /kPa	% cells plasmolysed			
	1	2	3	Mean
0	2	3	0	2.5
−500	34	40	38	37.3
−1000	58	60	59	59.0
−1500	70	78	64	70.1
−2000	97	89	93	93.0

Results: Look at the replicates in the results table and decide which water potential has the most similar and the most different results. Then state it like this:

The readings at −1000kPa are the most consistent because they are all close together. The mean at −1000kPa is therefore the most reliable.

The readings at −1500kPa are the least consistent as they have the greatest difference between so the mean at −1500kPa is the least reliable.

3. Use of error bars

If you have done a field work experiment where you are testing a correlation, you won't have precise replicates and so you can't draw error bars. You will need to explain why you do not have them and make a statement about how they can be used.

If you have an experiment with replicates, you can plot range bars or, with enough data, you can plot standard deviation or standard error bars. Just make sure you say which you have used. There are two ways you can use the bars and these relate to their length and to their overlap.

Range bar length

This is another way to think about consistency. The range bars show the highest and lowest readings and the mean falls between them. If the bar is short, then there is not much difference between the lowest and highest readings and so the readings are repeatable or consistent and so the mean is reliable. If the range bar is long, there is a big difference between the highest and lowest readings and so the readings are not repeatable or consistent and so the mean is not reliable. Look at your graph and decide which are the shortest and the longest range bars and use these to determine which are the most reliable and unreliable means.

Range bar overlap

This is all about how truly different the means are. The graph shown here has three data points. These are means and the range bars are plotted around them:

The range bars for A and B overlap. This is because the highest reading for A is higher than the lowest for B. This means that we do not have confidence that the means for A and B are truly different.

The range bars for A and C do not overlap because the lowest reading for A is higher than the highest for C. Therefore we have confidence that the mean for A is truly higher than the mean for C. The same is true for B and C: the mean for B is truly higher than the mean for C.

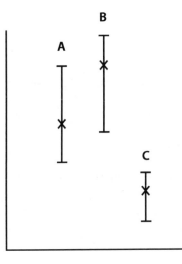

A word of warning: the raw data are fundamental. The raw data determine the length of the range bars. So when you write about this you must explain the logic the right way round. You can say 'the raw data are consistent therefore the range bars are small' NOT 'the range bars are small therefore the raw data are consistent'.

>> *Pointer*

If your mean does not seem to fall between your highest and lowest reading, you need to re-check your calculation. Some people have made that mistake. Don't be one of them.

>> *Pointer*

The overlap of the bars says NOTHING about repeatability; it tells you whether or not the means are truly different.

 Grade boost

When you are describing consistency there are two things you can talk about:

- Similarity in raw data.
- Length of range bars.

4. Uncertainty and improvement

This section is all about the inherent problems with your equipment or the design of your experiment. It is not about human error – the assumption is you know how to use all the apparatus and you make precise readings with no errors. You are perfect but the experiment is not.

When you have identified the areas that lead to lowered confidence in your results or decreased accuracy in your readings, you can suggest suitable improvements.

Subjective or objective?

The biggest source of error is subjectivity. This problem was considered in the context of experiment design on pages 42–43. A reading is subjective when you are making a value judgement such as timing exactly when the colour of methylene blue has gone or just how red the hydrogen carbonate indicator is. When making a subjective decision about timing, a more accurate stop clock won't help. You may be able to measure to 0.001s instead of 1s but as you are making the choice yourself when to stop the stop clock, the increased accuracy of the clock won't tell you more accurately when the colour has gone. A more useful improvement when judging a colour change is to use a colorimeter. You could, for example, time how long it takes for your solution to reach a pre-determined absorbance. Then, as you are reading numbers on a scale, there is no personal choice involved and so the reading is objective.

Counting

A similar source of error involves counting. It is possible to count incorrectly. A field work example is testing the effect of phosphate ion concentration on the number of water shrimp. If you have a lot of water shrimp in your river sample and they are swimming fast, it is very hard to count them. In this case an improvement is to take a representative volume of your sample, e.g. 100cm³ river water, and count how many water shrimp are there. Then measure the volume of your total sample and multiply up.

Accuracy of equipment

Your experiment may be entirely objective. In that case you must consider the accuracy of your equipment. Consider all the measurements you have made. They may include temperatures, volumes, lengths or masses. The source of uncertainty is derived from the accuracy of calibrations. This was discussed a bit in the section on decimal places in the results tables (pages 22–23) in relation to reading the scale on a thermometer. If the thermometer is calibrated in degrees, it is only accurate to 1C°. An improvement would be to have a thermometer which is calibrated to 0.1C°.

You can think about rulers and measuring cylinders in a similar way. A ruler may be calibrated in mm so to measure a length more accurately you could use callipers, calibrated to 0.1mm. But you may be measuring the diameter of bacterial colonies, in which case, callipers would not be suitable. Here, you could project an image of a known length on to a monitor and calculate its magnification. Then you project an image of the colony and measure the diameter of that. Use the calculated magnification of your known length to calculate the actual diameter if the colony. It would still be to the nearest mm but the larger the length you measure, the smaller the % error.

A measuring cylinder may be calibrated in cm³ so an improvement would be to use a burette, calibrated to 0.2cm³ or a syringe calibrated to 0.1cm³.

» Pointer

Objective is the opposite of subjective. An objective reading will be the same whoever makes it, whereas a subjective reading may depend on the person making it. Scientific method relies on people being able to repeat experiments, so objective measurements are essential.

» Pointer

Make sure you know the difference between subjective and objective readings. Make sure you know which yours are.

When measuring mass, your balance may be correct to the nearest 0.1g so a balance that measures to 0.01g would make the reading more accurate. Another way of improving mass measurements applies if you are using a top-pan balance. If someone walks by while you are using the balance, air movements may lift the balance pan. It may be too small an effect for you to see, but the effect will be to give you an artificially low mass. So an improvement would be to shield the balance from air movements.

Sources of error are obvious once you know how to look for them. In all these examples discussed above, the improvements could be worked out from a careful examination of your equipment. Your examiner is interested in your ideas about inaccuracy, rather than accuracy. So decide on the biggest source of error and describe it in detail. Give two examples of improvements to your experiment, one related to this major source of uncertainty and one other.

Pointer

Be realistic when deciding how many decimal places to use. You are not working on the Large Hadron Collider. Going to an accuracy of three decimal places in your equipment may not make the experiment any more accurate because of all the other sources of error.

Photosynthesis example

A popular experiment involves lining up vials of photosynthesising algae at various distances from a lamp. Major sources of error here are shading and, in the case of incandescent bulbs, differential heating effect from the lamp. The best solution to the shading problem is to do each vial separately. This takes much longer but this discussion is theoretical only, so that would be a valid improvement. If you have a fluorescent lamp, there should be no heat coming from the bulb, so that would be an improvement. Another way around this is to put a container of water between the lamp and the vials. This would absorb the heat and not the light. But take care. If you use a beaker of water, the lensing effect of the curved surface will alter the light intensity in different ways at different distances. If you are going to do this, you need a glass vessel with flat sides, like a chromatography tank.

Two field work examples

In a field work experiment using a t-test, you could explain that the use in Biology of the 0.05 probability contributes to your acceptance or rejection of the null hypothesis and so enhances the accuracy of your conclusion, compared with if you had used, say a 0.01 probability.

A suitable improvement for an experiment using a quadrat would be to ensure you have the right area quadrat. You would have to do this before you start the main experiment, and it is a small experiment in itself, as described on page 29.

What not to do:

- Do not suggest more replicates as an improvement. It is true that the more replicates you have, the more reliable the mean but this is about experimental technique and more replicates do not make your results or your conclusion any more accurate.

- Do not suggest more values for the independent variable unless you are trying to identify a special property of the system. Here are some special cases where more values of the independent variable are justified:

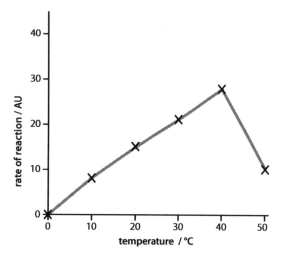

First example: If you are looking for an optimum value, e.g. when testing the effect of temperature on enzyme activity, your graph may look like the one on the left.

The optimum temperature for this reaction lies between 30°C and 50°C so an improvement would be to take more readings at temperatures between these two to more accurately find the optimum , e.g. 35°C, 38°C, 42°C and 45°C.

It would not be an improvement to take more readings below 30°C or above 50°C as that would not provide any useful information.

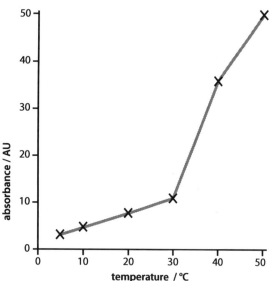

Second example: Some experiments produce a graph with a sudden gradient change; for example, looking at the permeability of beetroot membranes by assessing the absorption of pigment solutions leaked out after treatment in different temperatures. The graph may look like the one shown here.

The sharp gradient change represents a phase change in the membrane and you could improve the experiment by taking more readings around the temperature at which the gradient changes, to find that transition temperature more accurately. It will be between 20°C and 40°C so you could try 24°C, 28°C, 33°C and 37°C.

Third example: If the gradient were constant throughout, there would be no point in taking readings at more values of the independent variable within the range you have already covered. The only reason to do more values of the independent variable would be to extend the range if you had a good reason to think the gradient might change. If you were investigating the effect of substrate concentration on reaction rate, you might expect the rate to become constant when the enzyme is saturated. But the graph may not have reached a plateau at the substrate concentrations you have used, as shown here.

As an improvement it would be reasonable to try higher concentrations to find the substrate concentration that saturates the enzyme. So you might try $1.5\,mol\,dm^{-3}$, $1.75\,mol\,dm^{-3}$ and $2.0\,mol\,dm^{-3}$.

5. Explanation and relationship of results to theory

This is the biggest part of the analysis and it is where you show your examiner that you understand what you have done and its significance. Relate your own results to your theoretical expectations. Say if your results support the theory. Your results do not have to conform to theoretical expectations but you must be able to discuss them and try to explain them.

Your examiner will be looking for the major biological principles that underpin the experiment.

Some examples:

- If it is an experiment looking at the decolorisation of methylene blue by yeast, you must explain the biochemistry of both aerobic and anaerobic respiration. Both will be taking place unless you have made your solutions in boiled water and stored them under oil and performed the experiment in a nitrogen atmosphere.
- If your experiment tests the effect of light on photosynthesis, then you will need details of the light-dependent reaction of photosynthesis. You will need to explain the concept of limiting factors and how that applies in this case.
- An experiment testing the effect of antibiotics on bacteria will need a description of bacterial cell walls and the effects of antibiotics on them.
- A field work experiment will need to describe the niche of the organism under test and explain how its physiology or anatomy or behaviour is relevant to the independent variable you are testing. If you have tested the effect of light intensity or monitored it as a controlled variable, it is important to realise that it is not the light intensity here and now that matters. What is significant is the average light intensity over the whole of the growing season. All you can do is measure it on the day you do your experiment, but you have to use that as a proxy for the whole of the time the plant has been above ground.

If you have done an enzyme experiment, make sure you describe the reaction by giving an equation and explaining why it is physiologically important.

Use of language is very important here. Your choice of words must be such that your meaning is absolutely clear. You will find more ideas about clear writing on pages 73–74. Plan what you are going to write for this section and then divide it into paragraphs, where each paragraph contains one thought. Not only will it look more attractive, but it will show that you think in an organised fashion.

Grade boost

Remember to include an equation and description of the reaction in an enzyme experiment.

Grade boost

When you describe the theory that explains your experiment, relate it to your own results. Use phrases like, 'as can be seen from the graph ...' or 'the table shows ...' so your examiner knows that you are interpreting your own data.

6. Conclusion

This wraps up the whole experiment and brings together various strands. At its simplest, the conclusion is a statement of what you have learned, i.e. the trend you have observed and is an answer to the aim. Here are three examples:

Aim	Trend
To test the effect of temperature on the trypsin digestion of milk.	As the temperature increases, the time taken for trypsin to digest milk decreases up to 40°C. Above 40°C, the time increases.
To test the effect of carbon dioxide concentration on the rate of algal photosynthesis.	The rate of photosynthesis increases as the carbon dioxide concentration increases up to 0.05 mol dm^{-3}. Above this concentration, the rate decreases.
To test the effect of dissolved oxygen concentration on the number of mayfly nymphs.	As the concentration of dissolved oxygen increases, the number of mayfly nymphs increases.

But you have already written this at the beginning of your analysis, so the actual concluding paragraph needs more. The conclusion needs to take this trend and comment on it in relation to various other aspects that you have written about, e.g.

>> *Pointer*

The conclusion is a distillation of the main points of your analysis. Check you have at least three of the items mentioned in the list given here.

a) Refer back to the prediction you made at the start and say if it is supported.

b) Illustrate the trend by making a % calculation if you observed a particular increase or decrease.

c) Refer to the data.

d) Refer to the graph.

e) Refer to the explanation you have given.

f) Comment on the reliability.

g) Comment on the accuracy.

Further work

This section is short. You must imagine using the same general experimental techniques as the main experiment, so there is no need to write the method. There are three things to do:

1. Choose a new independent variable and make the statement 'the new independent variable is ...'.

> **Example**
>
> **Main aim:** to test the effect of lactase concentration on the rate of digestion of lactose.
>
> **Further work independent variable:** the new independent variable is the temperature.

If you have made an unsuitable choice, such as investigating the effect of the volume of buffer, you will lose this mark, so make sure your choice would provide meaningful information.

2. Choose two controlled variables and give their values. One could be the same as in the previous experiment but the other must be different. It is logical to make the second controlled variable the optimum value of the independent variable of your main experiment.

> **Example (as above)**
>
> **Main aim:** to test the effect of lactase concentration on the rate of digestion of lactose.
>
> **Further work independent variable:** the new independent variable is the temperature.
>
> **Controlled variables:**
>
> Lactase concentration at 20% of stock solution (found from main experiment to be suitable).
>
> Lactose concentration, using powdered milk at $4g/100cm^3$ solution (as in previous experiment).

3. Expected result – three things to think about here:
   a) A sentence to say what you think will happen.
   b) A sketch graph to illustrate your prediction.
   c) A brief explanation.

Example (as above)

Main aim: to test the effect of lactase concentration on the rate of digestion of lactose.

Further work independent variable: the new independent variable is the temperature.

Controlled variables:

Lactase concentration at 20% of stock solution (found from main experiment to be suitable).

Lactose concentration, using powdered milk at 4g/100cm³ solution (as in previous experiment).

Expected results:

a) As the temperature increases up to 30°C the reaction rate will increase. Above 30°C the reaction rate will decrease.

b) Sketch graph:

c) Increasing temperature increases the molecules' kinetic energy so more successful lactase-lactose collisions increase the rate of reaction. Above 30°C, the additional energy produces intramolecular vibrations which break hydrogen bonds maintaining the active site, the enzyme is denatured and so the reaction rate decreases.

Writing up checklist

This checklist shows all the items needed in your write up. You can't take this with you when you do your write up but in your booklet, you will find a list of headings. This list gives those headings with more detail so if you have thought hard about what is on this page, when it comes to writing up you will know what to do. The first part will seem like the design checklist. That's because you have to include a section about how your experiment was designed.

 Grade boost

Use this checklist with the Marking Criteria on pages 60 and 61 when you do practice write ups during the year.

Heading	Design area	Detail	I have done this
Aim	Aim	Clearly state aim in terms of two variables	
Prediction	Prediction	Describe what you think will happen stating the direction of change	
		Do not include any explanation	
Design	Independent variable	Clear statement to identify	
		Five values	
	Dependent variable	Clear statement to identify what is plotted	
		Units	
	Controlled variables	Decide the two most important and name them	
		Values for both, with units	
	Repeats	State how many; state it is to calculate mean for reliability	
	Control experiment	Identify which feature is inactivated	
		Identify what stays the same	
		If no suitable control explain why not and what control is for	
	Hazard	Identify hazard	
		Describe the risk	
		Describe how to minimise risk	
		Describe what to do if hazard occurs	
Results	Recording	Detailed column headings	
		Units in column headings only	
		Enough repeats or an explanation as to why not	
		Appropriate data recording to suitable number of decimal places	
	Graph	Both axes correctly labelled in detail	
		At least half page used for data points and line	
		Correct units on both axes	
		Suitable linear scale with a figure at the origin for both axes	
		Suitable break lines if necessary	
		All points plotted accurately and easily seen	
		Clear line joining points with no extrapolation	
		Error bars if appropriate	
	Statistics in some field work or genetics experiments	Explanation of why this test has been chosen	
		Null hypothesis	
		Correct calculation of test statistic	
		Number of degrees of freedom	
		0.05 level of significance or 95% confidence limits quoted	
		State critical value from tables	
		State whether calculated value is higher or lower than critical value	
		State whether null hypothesis accepted or rejected at 0.05 level of significance	
Analysis	Trend	Describe trend or explain the meaning of the statistical test	
	Consistency	How repeatable the raw data are	
	Error bars	Use of the error bars or standard deviation	
	Uncertainty	Major source of error in equipment or procedure explained or, for stats, explanation of level of significance	
	Improvements	Two improvements to the procedure explained	
	Explanation	Explain results coherently including major biological principles	
	Conclusion	Combine knowledge, prediction, results, accuracy, repeatability to make a valid conclusion	
Further work	Independent variable	State explicitly the new independent variable	
	Controlled variables	State two controlled variables and give the value for each	
	Expected results	State expected results, include a sketch graph and give a brief explanation	

5: How your experiment will be marked

If you have followed the instructions in the previous section, you will produce a report that conforms to what your examiner expects to see. The experiments for BY3 and BY6 are marked in a similar way. All the subheadings are the same. The difference is in the marking, not in what you do. This table shows you how the marking differs.

Marking criterion	BY3	BY6
Appropriate recording of results	1 mark	2 marks
Comment on use or suitability of error bars	–	1 mark
Explanation of results	5 marks	6 marks
Conclusion	1 mark	3 marks
Further work: expected results	1 mark	2 marks
Total marks for experiment	38	44

There are more marks available at BY6, which is consistent with work at A2 being more complex than work at AS.

Below are the marking criteria for BY3 and BY6 experiments. See how the marks in the column on the right relate to the checklist that appears in the writing up booklet. When you write up your experiment, you should keep referring to the checklist in the booklet. Reread the sections in this book which explain the criteria in detail. Then, when you come to write up your experiment, you will know exactly what to include.

>> Pointer

To get each mark, you must explain yourself very clearly and as fully as possible because your examiner cannot guess what you mean and cannot give you the benefit of the doubt if you haven't given enough detail.

Marking criteria for the BY3 experiment

Subheading	Mark point	Criterion	Marks
Aim/ prediction	Pa	Identify variables	1
	Pb	Link with direction	1
Design	Da	Identify independent variable	1
	Db	Give five values for independent variable	1
	Dc	State dependent variable and give units	1
	Dd	Name two controlled variables that are relevant	1
	Dd	Give values for the two controlled variables	1
	De	Repeats; calculate mean; increases reliability	1
	Df	Describe suitable control experiment or explanation why there isn't one	1
	Df	Refer to same conditions; explanation of use of a control	1
	Dg	Identify main hazards; how they may injure; procedure to minimise risk	1
Results	Ra	Correct title and column headings	1
	Rb	Units in column headings only	1
	Rc	Enough repeats or explanation why there were not enough	1
	Rd	Accuracy appropriate to instruments used/mean or rate calculations	1
Graph	Re	Axes correctly labelled	1
	Rf	Use at least half page for line	1
	Rg	Correct units on both axes	1
	Rh	Suitable linear scale including origin	1
	Ri	Points accurately plotted	2
	Rj	Suitable line joining points	1

Subheading	Mark point	Criterion	Marks
Analysis	Aa	Description of general trend shown by results	1
	Ab	Comment on consistency of raw data or use of range bars	1
	Ac	Comment on source of uncertainty	1
	Ad	Two suitable improvements to this experiment	2
	Ae	Explanation using biological knowledge; comparison with theoretical expectations	5
	Af	Conclusion	1
	Ag	Teacher's signature	1
Further work	Fa	Name a different independent variable	1
	Fb	Two appropriate controlled variables + a value for each	2
	Fc	Expected results	1
Total			**38**

Marking criteria for BY6

Subheading	Mark point	Criterion		Marks
Aim/ prediction	Pa	Identify variables		1
	Pb	Link with direction		1
Design	Da	Identify independent variable		1
	Db	Give five values for independent variable		1
	Dc	State dependent variable and give units		1
	Dd	Name two controlled variables that are relevant		1
	Dd	Give values for the two controlled variables		1
	De	Repeats; calculate mean; increases reliability		1
	Df	Describe suitable control experiment or explanation why there isn't one		1
	Df	Refer to same conditions; explanation of use of a control		1
	Dg	Identify main hazards; how they may injure; procedure to minimise risk		1
Results	Ra	Correct title and column headings		1
	Rb	Units in column headings only		1
	Rc	Enough repeats or explanation why there were not enough		1
	Rd	Accuracy appropriate to instruments used/mean or rate calculations		2
Graph or Statistics		**GRAPH**	**STATISTICS**	
	Re	Axes correctly labelled	Reason for choice of statistical test	1
	Rf	Use at least half page for line	Null hypothesis	1
	Rg	Correct units on both axes	Correct calculation of test statistic	1
	Rh	Suitable linear scale including origin	Number of degrees of freedom, level of significance or confidence limits quoted	1
	Ri	Points accurately plotted	Critical value quoted with statement that higher or lower than calculated value	2
	Rj	Suitable line joining points	Accept or reject null hypothesis at 0.05 level of significance	1
Analysis	Aa	Description of general trend shown by results		1
	Ab	Comment on consistency of raw data		1
	Ac	Comment on the use of the range bars		1
	Ad	Comment on source of uncertainty		1
	Ae	Two suitable improvements to this experiment		2
	Af	Explanation using biological knowledge; comparison with theoretical expectations		6
	Ag	Conclusion		3
	Ah	Teacher's signature		1
Further work	Fa	Name a different independent variable		1
	Fb	Two appropriate controlled variables + a value for each		2
	Fc	Expected results		2
Total				**44**

6: Looking at photographs

Biology is very visual so using photographs is a useful way of learning. A photograph may be used just to give you an image related to the subject matter, such as a portrait of Dolly the Sheep or a cactus. You may not have to use the photo in your answer but it helps you focus your thoughts.

Sometimes an examination question will ask you to provide evidence from a photograph, so you have to be careful that what you write actually refers to the picture, rather than what you assume is in it. You could be asked to give evidence from the photo of an advantage of fish farms. Now you can't see the individual fish so, even though you know it's true, you could not use 'no interspecific competition' as your answer, because you can't see which fish are there. But you could explain that having the fish farm closer to the shore than a fishing ground would reduce transport costs when the fish are caught.

You may be given a photomicrograph, i.e. a photograph taken down a microscope, or an electron micrograph, i.e. a photograph taken in an electron microscope. It could be a whole mount, i.e. a complete organism or it could be a thin section. If the electron micrograph were taken using a scanning electron microscope, you could be given a surface view. If the image is of cells, there are two ways you could be questioned. You may be asked to identify structures within a cell, so make sure you are used to looking at micrographs of cellular structures and that you can recognise them.

Or, given the magnification, you may be asked to calculate the length of one of the structures. The question will say 'show your working' so you must.

You may have an electron micrograph of a mitochondrion and be asked to calculate its actual length, given that it has been magnified 50,000 times.

Measure the mitochondrion's length. Let's say it is 55mm. As it has been magnified 50,000 times the image must be 50,000 times bigger than the real thing. So to find the actual size you divide the measured size by 50,000.

Always quote the formula:

$$\text{magnification} = \frac{\text{image size}}{\text{object size}}$$

Then substitute in the numbers:

$$\text{object size} = \frac{\text{image size}}{\text{magnification}}$$

$$= 55 \div 50,000\text{mm}$$

$$= 0.0011\text{mm}$$

This is the answer in mm, which is correct, and you must, of course, include the units. But 0.0011 is a very small number and so a more suitable unit would be microns. So the last lines of your calculation would be:

$$= 0.0011 \times 1000\mu$$

$$= 1.1\mu$$

Grade boost

Don't ever forget to put in the units.

It might be useful to use the triangle method to help you get the equation right:

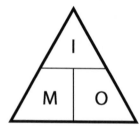

The triangle reminds you which way the equation works:

$I = M \times O$

$M = I/O$

$O = I/M$

I = image size
O = object size
M = magnification

When you have done a calculation, check that your answer is realistic and makes sense. In the example here, you might know that 1μ is about right for a mitochondrion. But if your answer turned out to be, say, 250μ, you would know that it was wrong, and so you would have to check your measuring and your working. Here are some sizes that are easy to remember.

>> Pointer

If you didn't know that mitochondria are about 1μ long, you could work out if it was a suitable answer. Since Year 7 you have known that cells are often about 1/30mm, which is about 30μ. You know how mitochondria look in relation to the whole cell, so that would tell you that 1μ is a suitable answer.

Very approximate lengths:

Structure	Length/μ
Animal cells	10–30
Plant cells	10–100
Nucleus	10

Structure	Length/μ
Chloroplast	5
Mitochondrion	2
Bacterium	3

7: Food tests

If you plan to be a biochemist, dietician or food technologist, one of your tasks may be to test foods to see what they are made of. You may have been doing this since Year 7 but at A Level it is much more interesting, even though the colour changes are still the same. There are four tests you have to know about and understand how to use. They are the tests for:

1. Reducing sugars
2. Non-reducing sugars
3. Proteins
4. Starch

Pointer

Make sure you know these four food tests: reducing sugars, non-reducing sugars, proteins and starch.

Pointer

All sugars are all white, crystalline, sweet-tasting and soluble in water. That is why we need tests to distinguish the different types.

Reducing sugars

This was probably introduced to you in Year 7 as the test for simple sugars, but the simple sugars it tests for, like glucose and fructose, all do the chemical process of reduction. It is this that produces the familiar colour change from blue to brick-red.

You are sometimes asked to describe how to do the test and, as this question could be worth three marks, you have to make three separate points. They are:

1. Mix the test solution with an equal volume of Benedict's reagent.
2. Heat the mixture in a water bath 70°C (or 80°C or 90°C or 100°C – it doesn't matter which as long as you state a temperature).
3. Observe the colour change from blue to orange (or red or 'brick-red').

Actually, when you do the test you will see that the colour the blue solution changes to depends on how concentrated the sugar solution is and how long you leave it. In fact, you could see a gradation from blue to murky green to orange to red to brown.

The colour comes from the reaction of the blue Cu^{2+} ion that gives the solution its blue colour. The sugar donates an electron to the copper ion and the ion is reduced to Cu^+. Donating an electron is a reduction so the sugar is a 'reducing sugar'. The reaction can be written like this:

$$Cu^{2+}_{(aq)} \quad + \quad e^- \quad \longrightarrow \quad Cu^+_{(s)}$$
$$\text{blue} \qquad \text{from sugar} \qquad \qquad \text{red}$$

The Benedict's test is sometimes described as being semi-quantitative. That means that you can tell which of various solutions has more or less reducing sugar in it and put them in relative order but you can't put a number on it. To do that, you would have to set up an experiment with different known glucose concentrations but keep everything else the same. Then you can use the final range of colours as a guide and match the colour given by the unknown concentration to a colour from a known concentration.

Grade boost

Remember that when you describe the test for reducing sugars, you must write 'Benedict's reagent + heat'. Don't forget the heat.

Pointer

The Cu^+ is in red copper oxide, Cu_2O, which precipitates out. It appears as a different colour depending on its concentration and the proportion of Cu^{2+} remaining.

Pointer

When you write about the Benedict's test, please give it a capital B, as it was invented by Mr Stanley Benedict from Cincinnati. And give it an apostrophe before the s because it is his test. It is not the Benedictine test and has nothing to do with monks distilling alcohol.

Non-reducing sugars

An examination question may ask about white, soluble crystals that do not give a red precipitate with Benedict's reagent. The question may ask how you would identify them. The first obvious thought is that they are sugar but health and safety concerns mean that you can't taste them. As they are not reducing sugar, the next logical step is to test for non-reducing sugar. This is what you do:

Grade boost

When you describe the conversion of disaccharides into monosaccharides, say they are hydrolysed, not broken down. It's always best to use the correct technical term.

1. To $2cm^3$ of the solution add two drops of the enzyme sucrase. Sucrase is supplied as a liquid, hence the units 'drops'.
2. Leave at room temperature for 5 minutes.
3. Add $2cm^3$ Benedict's reagent.
4. Incubate at 70–100°C for 10 minutes.
5. If the blue of the Benedict's reagent has changed colour, a reducing sugar has been produced by the sucrase. This indicates that the sucrase had been acting on a non-reducing sugar. If the original non-reducing sugar had been sucrose, this is what has happened:

$$\underset{\textit{non-reducing sugar}}{\text{sucrose + water}} \xrightarrow{\textit{sucrase}} \underset{\textit{reducing sugars}}{\text{glucose + fructose}} \xrightarrow{\textit{Benedict's reagent/heat}} \text{red precipitate}$$

Some textbooks will tell you to hydrolyse the sucrose with hydrochloric acid by boiling the sucrose and acid together for 10 minutes. Then, in order to do the Benedict's test, you have to neutralise the acid with sodium hydrogen carbonate and keep testing with indicator paper until you achieve pH7. Using sucrase is quicker, more reliable, works at a lower temperature and allows you to deal with much smaller volumes of liquid.

But to return to the examination question, if you did not get a red precipitate after sucrose treatment, then you are not dealing with a sugar. The next step in the logic requires you to do the Biuret test for molecules with peptide bonds, i.e. proteins and peptides.

Something to try at home: drink some cold lemonade. It tastes sweet, because of the sucrose, and sharp, because of the citric and carbonic acids. Heat some and cool it again before tasting. Now it tastes like honey. This shows two biochemical points:

- Sucrose breaks down into glucose and fructose, the main sugar in honey.
- Sucrose is hydrolysed by acid:

$$\text{sucrose} \xrightarrow{\text{\textit{carbonic acid}}} \text{glucose} + \text{fructose}$$

Biuret test

Make sure you can spell Biuret. It is purple and made by a chemical reaction when you test for a protein. Do not confuse it with burette, which is long, thin and made of glass.

When you are asked to describe this test in an examination, it could be worth three marks, so make sure you give at least three separate statements:

1. Mix equal volumes (e.g. 2cm³) of the solution you are testing with 1 mol dm⁻³ sodium hydroxide. You don't need to remember the concentration but if you give it, you are signalling to your examiner that you really know this.

2. Hold the test tube at an angle and gently trickle down the side of the test tube 10 drops 1% copper sulphate solution.

dropping pipette

test tube

10 drops CuSO$_4$

2cm³ test solution + 2 cm³ NaOH

•••**Practical tip**•••

Holding the test tube at an angle allows the copper sulphate to trickle gently down the side of the test tube. This means it will form a layer on the top and not mix into the test solution.

3. Where the copper sulphate meets the sodium hydroxide there is a reaction making blue copper hydroxide:

$$2NaOH + CuSO_4 \xrightarrow{\hspace{2cm}} \underset{\textit{blue}}{Cu(OH)_2} + Na_2SO_4$$

The copper hydroxide sits on the surface because you have trickled in the copper sulphate so gently, which is why this is sometimes called the 'blue ring test'. This happens whatever is in the test solution. It is the next step that proves you have peptide bonds present.

4. Cover the top of the test tube, invert it once and bring it back to a vertical position. If a protein is present, the blue colour will have disappeared and the solution will be purple. The purple compound is Biuret.

The Biuret test is another semi-quantitative test. The more protein there is, the darker the purple colour will be. If you have different shades of purple, you can put your test solutions in order of increasing concentration.

If you do the test with several solutions of known concentration, as long as all other factors stay the same, you can compare the purple they produce with the colour given by a solution of unknown concentration, and therefore, estimate the concentration of your unknown.

Starch test

This is another test that you probably learned in Year 7. In those days you would have said that starch makes iodine go blue-black. It's still broadly true, but at A Level there is more to say about it.

First of all, at room temperature, iodine is a deep purple, crystalline solid. This test uses a solution of iodine in potassium iodide, so the important ion in this reaction is I_3^-. The I_3^- ion made like this: $KI + I_2 \longrightarrow K^+ + I_3^-$. This is why we refer to 'iodine solution' rather than just 'iodine' at A Level.

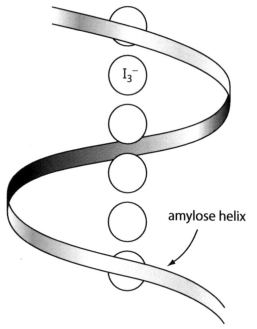

I_3^-

amylose helix

The type of starch that this ion identifies is amylose, which, as you may remember from unit BY1, is an α-helix of α-1,4 linked glucose molecules. The diagram shows how the I_3^- ion is held within the helix and it is the interaction of its electrons with the electrons of the amylose helix that produces the colour change:

The iodine solution is brown and the starch–iodide complex looks mauve, purple, blue-black or black, depending on its concentration.

Two factors affect this test:

- pH – low pH hydrolyses the starch, so the iodine test cannot be done in those conditions.

- Temperature – the amylose molecules and iodide ions have kinetic energy and are constantly moving. At room temperature, their movement is not enough to disrupt the complex. But if you put the test tube into a water bath to heat the complex, the kinetic energy of the I_3^- ions is enough to make it leave the starch helix and so the blue-black colour disappears. If you take the test tube out of the water bath again, you can probably guess what happens to the colour.

This test is often used to show the rate at which amylase digests starch. You will see that on page 33.

Summary of tests

Learn these colour changes by heart as examinations questions often ask you to state what they are.

Test for	Reagents	Initial colour	Colour of positive result
reducing sugars	Benedict's	blue	red
non-reducing sugars	hydrolysis + Benedict's	blue	red
protein	sodium hydroxide and copper sulphate	blue ring	purple
starch	iodine solution	red-brown	blue-black

Food tests checklist

Topic	Detail	I know this
All sugars	What are the physical properties of all sugars?	
Reducing sugars	Which test?	
	What reagents are needed?	
	How is the test done?	
	What is the colour change for a positive result?	
Non-reducing sugars	Which test?	
	What reagents are needed?	
	How is the test done?	
	What is the colour change for a positive result?	
Proteins	Which test?	
	Which bond does this test for?	
	What reagents are needed?	
	How is the test done?	
	What is the colour change for a positive result?	
Starch	Which test?	
	What reagents are needed?	
	How is the test done?	
	What is the colour change for a positive result?	
	What can you say about the temperature for the test to work?	
	What can you say about the pH for the test to work?	

8: Using whole organs and organisms

1. Use of animal dissection

You don't actually have to do dissection for A Level Biology. Some people say 'I'm too squeamish' and don't like to even think about it. Even people who say they want to be a doctor or a dentist say that, and if you are one of those people, you may wish to consider another profession.

Some people say, 'I don't want to dissect because I'm a vegetarian'. You won't be eating it, so that argument doesn't work.

Some people say, 'It's cruel' but the reality is that the animals that are dissected in schools and universities are housed in clean, safe conditions where they have appropriate food and drink and live an infection- and predator-free environment. They live longer, healthier lives than would ever occur in the wild. If you are to dissect an organ rather than a whole animal, the organ would come from a butcher and so the animal from which it came is subject to all the laws governing the food industry.

Dissection is a wonderful way to learn. You can look at all the photos you like, read all the books, watch all the YouTube dissections and simulations you can find, but to do it yourself, you will learn the feel – the resilience of adipose tissue, the flexibility of blood vessels, the strength of the heart tendons and so on.

So take advantage when material is made available for you to dissect. At least watch what is going on or, if you prefer to watch at one step removed and use your phone to film your friend doing the work and then watch it on the screen later. It's never as good though. If you have dissected, you will have something to discuss at an interview and you will show yourself to be a committed student who has gained first-hand knowledge of how organisms are structured.

You are likely to be offered to dissect mammalian organs such as the kidney and the heart. You may also dissect fish gills. In this case, ask your teacher to show you how to expose the brain and ask how to extract the eye and you can dissect that, especially if it is a large fish, such as a salmon. Take out the lens, clean it and read through it. You may also have the chance to dissect an earthworm or locust or possibly larger animals such as dogfish, frog, rat or rabbit. Use every learning opportunity you can.

●●●Practical tip●●●

If you like dissecting hearts or kidneys you can buy them at the butcher's and have a go at home. Try the liver as well. Go to the fish counter and buy a whole fish, such as a herring, to dissect its gut, gills and brain. Maybe, in the interests of education, the fishmonger will give you a fish head that the previous customer didn't want.

2. Whole plants, fruits and seeds

In the section of the specification in BY5 about plant reproduction, you are required to know about wind- and insect-pollinated plants. The best way to support what you learn about this from the textbook is to examine flowers. Some people find plants boring, but that is usually because they haven't learned much about them. Just because they do not have scales, fangs or venom doesn't mean they can't wage war and protect themselves. Plants are fascinating.

Look at the flower structures so you really know what the 'small, green inconspicuous petals' of wind-pollinated flowers actually look like. Look at different types of flower so you can see anthers within insect-pollinated flowers, as opposed to anthers held outside wind-pollinated flowers by their long filaments. Actual flowers look different from models and diagrams, so make sure you look at real ones and that you look at as many different species as you can.

•••Practical tip•••

While you are working at home, raid the fridge, fruit bowl, vegetable rack and garden. Ask for permission, then dissect any plant material you find. Not only will it help you understand their structures, you can eat them afterwards.

3. Use of models

When your teacher went to school, there were not many models available. Your teacher probably learned largely from textbooks. But you can relate what you learn in a textbook to a model which gives you the 3D version and so you understand so much better. You can see, for example, why the eye has a blind spot or why diffusion through the large air spaces in the spongy mesophyll of a leaf is efficient.

A model will help you learn a diagram, so if you are learning, for example, about the excretory system in mammals, improve your understanding of the diagrams by looking at a torso model and see how the components of the system are positioned in the body. See which kidney is higher.

Look at a flower model and understand the long distance the pollen tube has to grow. See the micropyle and understand that the pore remains when the integuments harden into the testa of the seed.

Grade boost

Look at a model of the pelvic area and see why a transplanted kidney is placed there rather than in the original position of the kidneys.

4. Use of preserved specimens

Part of your specification gives details of the classification you need to know. You will need to know the physical features that distinguish kingdoms and phyla and, in some cases, lower taxa such as class. Look at the specimens because it is these that will allow you to understand the features of less common organisms.

•••Practical tip•••

Study carefully the soft body and segmentation in Annelids; take note of the chitinous exoskeleton of Arthropods and note the number of pairs of walking legs in each class. Look at the lack of symmetry of Molluscs. This will help you understand and remember your taxonomy.

9: Use of resources

You may have heard of the advice given to students in the United States when they have a problem with their work. Apply the four Bs in this order:

1. Brains (the most complex object in the known universe and we all have one).
2. Books (although now that includes all print and electronic media).
3. Buddies (our friends may know the answer but these days we are very conscious of the moral problems of copying and plagiarism, so take care how you use their work and ideas).
4. Boss (your teacher).

This section explores 2, i.e. the books, journals, websites and videos that you have access to. If you go straight to 4 and ask for an answer, the answer is all you have. If you look it up for yourself, you have the answer but you also have the intellectual development that got you there as well as all the snippets of information you picked up on the way. This is the beginnings of the differences between information, knowledge and wisdom. We would all like wisdom but you have to work for it.

There are many ways to acquire information and people learn best when they have identified their own preference. Using different types of learning for different types of knowledge is useful and the more ways you approach something, the more chance you have of finding the way that appeals to you. So don't use just one book or website or buddy. Try several and generate the answer that makes most sense to your way of thinking.

Books

Books for A Level students are at the right depth and have been written with A Level specifications in mind. This is why it is often much easier to find what you need at the right level in a book rather than on the Internet.

There are many excellent general Biology textbooks but you are lucky to have books dedicated to this WJEC A Level course and you are advised to use them, among others. Always use the dedicated books and at least one other in addition to study guides. The more times you read something, the easier it will be to understand. These books by Gareth Rowlands, published by Illuminate Publishing, are a good place to start:

WJEC AS Biology

WJEC A2 Biology

WJEC AS Biology Study and Revision Guide

WJEC A2 Biology Study and Revision Guide

To help with drawings

Freeman and Bracegirdle, *An Atlas of Histology*, pub Heinemann Educational 1968

Freeman and Bracegirdle, *An Advanced Atlas of Histology*, pub Heinemann 1976

Bracegirdle and Miles, *Atlas of plant structure Vol I*, pub Heinemann Educational 1971

Bracegirdle and Miles, *Atlas of plant structure Vol II*, pub Heinemann Educational 1973

Shaw, Lazell and Foster, *Photomicrographs of flowering plant*, pub. Longman 1965

Shaw, Lazell and Foster, *Photomicrographs of non-flowering plant*, pub Longman 1968

Websites

Make a habit of checking www.wjec.co.uk for specific information about the course you are taking. Use other websites with care. Many standard experiments are performed and discussed online. There are of course dedicated revision websites as well as websites devoted to single aspects of the course. Use these wisely and remember that just because you have seen it online, it doesn't make it true or correct and it doesn't necessarily mean it has been explained to a suitable depth for A Level students.

Use a search engine to find the organ or organism you would rather not dissect or the experiment you need help understanding. Or try these:

Simulations: many people do not want to dissect material of animal origin, indeed it is not even required at some medical schools. Instead students use web-based simulations. Some even have sound effects.

Salmon dissection. tinyurl.com/cmlg7rx

Frog dissection. tinyurl.com/aa4f7k and www.froguts.com

Videos: once students can overcome their yuk factor, watching videos can be very useful because they are made to enhance the important aspects. YouTube is full of eyes, hearts, kidneys and so on. The theory has so much more meaning when you have seen the real thing.

Heart dissection instructions and video. tinyurl.com/blvkmjd

Cow eye dissection video. tinyurl.com/cg7gpdg

Kidney dissection. tinyurl.com/d4htx73

Genetics simulation: try this exercise on the genetics of dragons to enhance your understanding of genotype and phenotype, dominant and recessive alleles and sex linkage. tinyurl.com/d8byhsr

Journals

Biological Sciences Review is published by Philip Allan four times a year. It is aimed specifically at A Level students and has well-written and well-illustrated articles about topics in Biology and also has articles referring to examination technique.

NewScientist has excellent articles and even if you find it all too much, at least read the table of contents so that you know what is going on in the world of science, and look at the cartoons.

10: Use of language, spelling, punctuation and grammar

When you write under exam conditions it is most important that what you write is what you mean and that it is understood by your examiner to be what you mean. Scientific terminology is useful because the technical words have specific meanings which are unambiguous. In addition to the specialist vocabulary, your normal use of English must also convey exactly what you mean.

Spelling

Pointer

Language changes over time, but at any one time, a spelling is generally either right or wrong. It's better to be right.

Spelling must be accurate because there are many similar words with quite different meanings. Thymine and thiamine are two very different molecules. Meiosis and mitosis are quite different processes. Kew Gardens is not spelled Cue. In field work, you use a quadrat, not a quadrant. Your examiner will give you the benefit of the doubt in many cases, but where there are such similar words to distinguish, the spelling must be accurate.

Punctuation

Punctuation is important. Sometimes people write a whole page with no full stops and no capital letters. It is not up to the examiner to work out where your sentences begin and end. Keep your sentences short, avoid sub-clauses and you will not lose track of your thoughts.

Pronouns

Pointer

Take care when you use pronouns, especially 'it'.

A pronoun technically refers to the preceding noun. Sometimes people think faster than they write and use the word 'it' without realising the noun it refers to is so far back that the sentence becomes meaningless. Unless you are most confident, avoid the word 'it'. Your examiner will not try to guess what 'it' means. Your meaning must be clear.

Apostrophes

Pointer

Remember it's = it is; its is possessive.

Many people do not realise that an apostrophe can mean that a letter has been left out, e.g. 'don't' means 'do not'. A common error in this connection is the word 'its'. With an apostrophe, it's, it means it is. The i has been left out. Without the apostrophe 'its' is possessive, e.g. Look at the sky. Its colour is blue.

An apostrophe is not used when you make a plural, e.g. one dog, two dogs.

Clichés

Avoid clichés. Depending on your experiment, you may tend to slip into common phrases that are often a substitute for thought, such as 'playing God', 'slippery slope' and 'designer babies', although these particular examples are unlikely to crop up in your write up.

Miscellaneous misuse

- The word 'amount' is a problem. It has many meanings including mass, concentration, number and volume. So if you find yourself writing the word 'amount' cross it out immediately and write the word you really mean. The only exception to this rule is when you are discussing trampling.
- Another word to avoid is 'things'. It's far too vague and suggests you haven't bothered to think through carefully enough what you actually mean.
- Remember that you put your solutions in test tubes, not in testubes.
- You will write the word dependent and independent many times throughout your A Level career. Make sure the third letter from the end is an e.
- If you have a controlled variable, a factor is kept constant and so you control it. But a control experiment shows that it is the independent variable that is causing the change in the dependent variable. Do not confuse control and controlled.
- When you are using very hot water you have a hazard because it could burn your skin. But it will scald you, not scold you. Many people seem to think the water will tell them off.
- If you want to assess the colour of a liquid, use a colorimeter, not a calorimeter.
- This is Britain. If you use Americanisms but your meaning is clear, you will not be penalised. However, you are trying to write a well-produced piece of English prose so use English as spoken in this country. 'Got' not 'gotten', 'colour' not 'color', 'transport' not 'transportation', 999 not 911.

Handwriting

Your examiner will have hundreds of scripts to mark. The examiner is on your side and wants to give you marks but if your writing is illegible, however brilliant your work, you cannot get marks for it. Please take care. For example, make sure you distinguish a from o, otherwise lactase looks like lactose and it is not up to your examiner to guess which you mean. Cross each t and dot each i. Put spaces between words. Look at a Year 1 writing book and practise the exercises you haven't thought about for twelve years. You know it makes sense.

>> *Pointer*

A beautifully written script with perfect spelling and punctuation and every paragraph separate and distinct is all that is needed.

Little messages

Some candidates write a little note to the examiner at the end. It is not necessary to write, 'Thank you for marking my script', although we appreciate the gesture. It is not appropriate, however, to tell us your life story, girl-friend problems or information about your hangover. Stick to the Biology.

Glossary

Sometimes an exam question will ask about practical work. You may get a question that starts 'What is the meaning of the term …?' This glossary gives concise meanings of many of the technical terms used in practical work.

Section	Term	Meaning
Microscopy	Magnification	Ratio of image size : object size
	Resolution	Smallest distance between two points that can be distinguished
	Calibration	Calculation of actual length of scale on eyepiece graticule at a given objective lens magnification
	Graticule	Scale mounted inside eyepiece
	Stage micrometer	Slide accurately ruled showing sub-divisions of a 1cm line
	smu	Stage micrometer unit
	epu	Eyepiece unit; graduation on eyepiece graticule
	Photomicrograph	Photograph taken down a microscope
	Electron micrograph	Photograph taken using an electron microscope
How to design lab experiments	Variable	A factor that may change
	Independent variable	A factor chosen to change; values decided by experimenter
	Dependent variable	Measured, counted or calculated factor, the value of which depends on the independent variable
	Controlled variable	A factor that is kept constant throughout the experiment, so that only the independent variable is allowed to change prior to measuring the value of the dependent variable
	Control experiment	Experiment with major factor inactivated to demonstrate its significance in generating change in the dependent variable
	Accurate	True
	Repeatable	Reliable; consistent; readings are close to one another
	Reproducible	Experiment can be set up another way and get the same results
	Q_{10}	Rate of reaction at $(t+10)°C$/rate of reaction at $t°C$
	R_f	Distance moved by pigment/distance moved by solvent front
Approaches to field work	Sampling	Selection of individuals from a population to estimate the characteristics of the whole population
	Quadrat	A frame, often $0.25m^2$ square, open or gridded, for sampling organisms
	Transect	A line or belt along which organisms are identified, to contribute to defining the characteristics of a habitat
	Density	Number of organisms per m^2 on land or per m^3 in water
	% cover	% area occupied by a given species